the BEGINNER'S
guide to WICCA

the BEGINNER'S guide to WICCA

A practical guide for those starting on their Wiccan path

KIRSTEN RIDDLE

CICO BOOKS
LONDON NEW YORK

This edition published in 2020 by CICO Books
An imprint of Ryland Peters & Small Ltd
20–21 Jockey's Fields   341 E 116th St
London WC1R 4BW   New York, NY 10029

www.rylandpeters.com

10 9 8 7 6 5

First published in 2014

Text © Kirsten Riddle 2014
Design, illustration, and photography © CICO Books 2014

A CIP catalog record for this book is available from the Library of
Congress and the British Library.

ISBN: 978-1-78249-839-1

Printed in China

Editor: Rosie Lewis
Designer: Elizabeth Healey
Illustrators: Michael A. Hill and Trina Dalziel

Commissioning editor: Kristine Pidkameny
Art director: Sally Powell
Production controller: Mai-Ling Collyer
Publishing manager: Penny Craig
Publisher: Cindy Richards

MIX
Paper from
responsible sources
FSC® C106563

contents

Introduction: What is Wicca?

The Wiccan way is a powerful one. It's a peaceful path that can enhance life and help you to connect with the energies around you. It's a belief system that can lead you to greater appreciation of the beauty of Mother Earth and your own innate power. Do you enjoy watching the sun rise in the morning? Does it lift your heart and give you a sense that there's more to life? Maybe the moon inspires and captivates you. Perhaps you love spending time by the sea and soaking up the serenity of your surroundings. If this sounds like you, then you're already walking the path, learning to look a little deeper and tapping into the energy of the earth. A witch follows her intuition. She knows how to read the signs and symbols in the environment. It's not called the craft of the wise for nothing!

Sometimes referred to as the oldest religion, Wicca, or witchcraft as it is commonly called, has been around for centuries, passed down through families who shared their knowledge and experience. In the early days, being a witch meant being called on to heal the sick, dispense sage words and prophecies, and aid in everything from childbirth to a broken heart. Today, the role is not dissimilar. A witch is a healer, a leader, the kind of person you can go to for help and advice. She knows the power of words and how to help others make the most of their situation and manifest the things they need. She'll encourage and motivate and always endeavor to make things better. Interestingly, much of the misconception of witches was historically down to the fact that most were female, so they had monthly cycles. To the male of the species during medieval times, this was both strange and alarming—how could a woman bleed for a week and still be alive? To explain it, men created the idea that women had magical powers and that they were at their most potent during that time of the month. This is why many medieval spells, particularly those supposedly recorded during the witch trials, involved the use of menstrual blood.

MISUNDERSTANDINGS AND MISCONCEPTIONS

Despite ancient beliefs that tried to link witchcraft with black magic and wicked deeds, the Wiccan way is not and never has been evil. It's about feeling love for all things, caring for the community and the environment, and taking responsibility for your actions. In previous times, the Christian Church tried to portray Wicca as evil in an attempt to convince followers of the old ways to convert to its religion. Ironically, those who practice witchcraft don't consort with the Devil, because they don't believe in him. The Devil is a Christian invention, and a way to scare folk into the religion.

During the witch trials, many hundreds of innocent people were tortured and killed, simply for being different. If they had some knowledge of herbs or healing, then they were considered to be dangerous, or—in the case of many women—if they were spinsters it meant that there must be something supernatural about them. Thankfully, this is no longer the case, but there are still those who believe that witchcraft is satanic. Ironically, those who follow its path tend to be more self-aware, because they take responsibility for their thoughts, actions, and deeds. A true witch would never do anything that would harm or manipulate another person, because Wiccans believe that whatever they do in the world will return to them threefold. In other words, it makes sense to be loving and kind, because the universe responds by sending love and kindness by the bucketful. However, if you go through life thinking horrible thoughts and being unpleasant, it stands to reason that you'll attract a similar reaction from those around you, and your world will seem a dark and gloomy place. It's like choosing to walk on the sunny side of the street. It's all about perspective and learning to see things differently, and Wiccans tend to see the bigger picture and look on the bright side. As the famous phrase goes, "When life hands you lemons, make lemonade."

LEARNING FROM MOTHER NATURE

This is not to say that following this path means you'll always be full of the joys of spring, because life is full of ups and downs. But Wiccans understand the cycles of life. By learning from Mother Nature and the changing of the seasons, they understand that there must be periods of darkness as well as light, and that you have to embrace both, and learn to go with the flow. Valuable lessons about life can be learned by looking at and listening to the landscape. Wiccans also learn to read the energy of their own body. It is this kind of wisdom that is essential to the craft. Being open to whatever life throws at you, and giving thanks for your blessings, is another key element of witchcraft. Every living thing has a lesson to teach and something to offer.

So if you're looking for a way to move forward with optimism, make the most of your life, and help and care for others, then the Wiccan path could be the one for you. There are no restrictions apart from the ones you set yourself, and the only real rules are to harm no one and to take responsibility for your actions. The idea that witchcraft is about casting terrible curses is anathema to most Wiccans, who realize that anything negative will rebound on them. As with anything else, it is down to the practitioners and their state of mind at the time of performing any magical spells. This is why it is always a good idea to question your motives and to do some sort of cleansing ritual before practicing magic.

DISCOVERING THE MAGIC AROUND YOU

If you choose to learn more about this way of life, you'll see bountiful benefits. You'll start to notice magic in everything around you: in every tiny exchange or conversation, in the gifts and talents with whichc you're blessed. You'll look at the world through fresh eyes and see the power at your fingertips. You'll develop self-belief and confidence, and your energy levels will increase as you learn to read your own body and work with nature. You'll feel inspired and empowered to try different things and get to know new people. And you'll realize what a magnificent and truly amazing world we live in. If this sounds like your cup of tea, read on. If it doesn't, read on anyway, with an open mind and heart, and you may yet be pleasantly surprised.

How to Use this Book

Although the chapters are set out to give you the basics and provide you with an insight into the craft, you don't have to read them in a particular order. This is the kind of book you can dip in and out of. For example, you might feel immediately drawn to the section on Moon Magic, so follow your intuition and feel free to start there and work backward (by the way, walking backward in magical terms is called "widdershins" and is used in many protection spells). If you prefer to take a more ordered approach, start at the beginning and read a bit every day. The spells, suggestions, and rituals are based on traditional folklore and magic, but they're not set in stone. They're there to give you an idea of what you can do. Magic is personal, and you will create your own path, so take what you want and adapt it. Use this book as a guide or a starting point, as much or as little as you feel is right. The Wiccan path is about having the freedom to do what you want, in the way you want.

Finally, have fun. Wicca is not a morbid practice, and it's not about following things to the letter and worrying if you get something wrong. Consider nature: she grows and goes her own way; sometimes things work out, sometimes they don't and she creates a new way. But everything she does is beautiful, special, and unique—just like you and your magical endeavors. Being serious in your passion and commitment doesn't mean you have to be solemn. As any witch worth her salt will tell you, a smile is one of the most magical tools at your disposal, because it's filled with emotion, intent, and positive energy, and you can see the effect on others instantly. So enjoy the magical journey, and happy reading!

What kind of witch are you?

For a fun way to discover your true witchy nature and to help identify magical areas of interest, try this simple quiz. Just count the letter you ticked the most and read on to see what kind of witch you are.

1) You often make wishes:

a) At night under a full moon
b) When you're cooking up a storm in the kitchen
c) By lighting a candle
d) When you're out in the garden

2) Which three words best describe your personality?

a) Sensitive, creative, and intuitive
b) Warm, generous, and caring
c) Spontaneous, passionate, and enthusiastic
d) Practical, mystical, and earthy

3) To de-stress, you:

a) Take a stroll by the sea with the one you love
b) Get together with friends and family for a feast
c) Don your party dress and tear up the dance floor
d) Go for a picnic in the woods

4) Which of these workshops would you be drawn to?

a) Astrology
b) Everyday spellcraft
c) Fire-walking
d) Holistic remedies

5) TO GIVE YOURSELF A CONFIDENCE BOOST BEFORE A BIG EVENT, YOU:

a) Focus on your breathing
b) Remind yourself how amazing you are
c) Do some exercise
d) Make a soothing herbal brew

6) WHAT'S YOUR FAVORITE TYPE OF RESTAURANT?

a) A seafood restaurant
b) A traditional all-American diner
c) A tapas restaurant
d) A French bistro

7) YOUR FAVORITE MYTHOLOGICAL CREATURE IS:

a) A werewolf
b) A griffin
c) A dragon
d) A unicorn

8) WHICH QUALITY IS MOST IMPORTANT TO YOU IN A RELATIONSHIP?

a) Romance
b) Honesty
c) Passion
d) Friendship

9) YOU'RE AT YOUR HAPPIEST WHEN YOU ARE:

a) Sitting out under the stars at night
b) Decorating your boudoir
c) Gazing into an open fire
d) Learning something new

Mostly As
MOON WITCH

A sensitive soul who finds it easy to empathize with others, you're a Moon Witch at heart. Most at home under the stars, you have a vivid imagination. You're drawn to rituals that involve the phases of the moon and the planets, and you have a natural aptitude for astrology. Bodies of water also fascinate you, and you find it easy to relax by the sea. You're at your most powerful during the moon's waxing phase (when it gets bigger), so use this time to manifest the things you want, and to inspire others.

WICCAN WISDOM

Leave a glass of water outside during the night of the full moon. Use it as a rinse in the shower in the morning to give your energy a boost.

Mostly Bs
KITCHEN WITCH

Warm and kind-hearted, you love to put a smile on people's faces. Most at home when you're rustling up a sumptuous meal, you're a true Kitchen Witch. You know the power that you have at your fingertips, and how to use everyday items and ingredients to achieve your magical aims. Wise and knowledgeable, you easily draw people to you, which means you're constantly on call for advice. You have a natural flair for flavors and putting things together to create a masterpiece. Because of this, you'll be an adept spell–creator and–caster.

WICCAN WISDOM

A meal is like a spell, so whilst you're cooking, visualize your aim and say a few words, such as "This meal is made. My aim is true. Success is mine in all I do."

Mostly Cs
ELEMENTAL WITCH

Fiery and passionate, you're a changeable soul ruled by your emotions, so you'll make an excellent Elemental Witch. You embrace new things, and have an adventurous streak. You'll probably find that the weather affects your moods. You're vibrant, confident, and in tune with your body, and have an immense amount of energy, which you put to good use. Fast action suits you, so you'll naturally be drawn to fire and candle magic. You're at your most powerful when you're taking the lead, and, like the flames of a fire, you easily light up a room.

WICCAN WISDOM

When you need to feel super-empowered, imagine there's a flame in the center of your chest. Watch it grow to full height, filling you with strength and confidence.

Mostly Ds
HEDGE WITCH

A true earth mother, you feel a deep connection to nature, which makes you the perfect Hedge Witch. With a broad knowledge of plants and herbs, you'll love getting your hands dirty. An excellent communicator with strong creative skills, you have a natural way with words. You're adept at most types of healing; spells, charms, brews, and potions fascinate you, and you're constantly gathering information. A keen interest in folklore means that you enjoy mixing old traditions with new ideas. You feel most at home outdoors, and at your most powerful when surrounded by wildlife and cocooned by trees.

WICCAN WISDOM

To feel instantly rejuvenated, take your shoes off and go outside barefoot. Stand for a few minutes and enjoy the sensations as you connect with the earth.

CHAPTER 1

TOOLS, ESSENTIALS, SIGNS, AND SYMBOLS

Getting Started

Taking your first steps on the Wiccan path can be confusing. What do you need to know? How do you approach the subject of magic? And what about spells? You might feel as though you're overloaded with information. The important thing is to take your time. This is a journey of self-discovery, so enjoy it. Read and absorb, and start with something simple, like a ritual to awaken your spiritual self (see page 17). Incorporate small blessings into your life every day, and make a point of connecting with nature by getting to know the changes of each season, and learning how your pagan ancestors worked with these cycles. Give yourself time to adjust to new ideas and give thanks for any surprises along the way. Magic is about recognizing the wonder around you, about taking joy from the little things and passing it on. Start with what you're interested in. If you have a passion for the night sky, look into the cycles of the moon and how they might affect you and those around you. If you're drawn to plants and herbs, make this your starting point, and discover how you can use them to help yourself and others. Follow your heart and go with what gives you the greatest amount of joy—everything else will come naturally.

WICCAN WISDOM

Keep a journal of your discoveries, noting any interesting bits of information you uncover, as well as your thoughts and feelings.

AWAKEN YOUR SPIRITUAL SELF

Light a white candle to represent your spiritual self. Sit in front of the candle and breathe deeply. Imagine a spark inside your belly. See it grow into a flame that stretches upward and out of the top of your head. Now imagine that your spiritual essence, your soul, is traveling along the flame until it is outside of your body. Imagine that you can see above your head and move freely. You are floating in the air, so explore this sense of freedom and enjoy feeling as light as a feather. When you're ready, slip back into your body through the top of your head. Breathe and focus on your belly. Feel the warmth of the flame fill you up. You might want to say an affirmation, such as "I am a spiritual being, made of light and love."

CREATING A SACRED SPACE

Following the Wiccan path is a lifestyle choice. You incorporate it into your daily schedule by the way you think and act. In other words, it becomes second nature for you to consider the environment, work with energy, and embrace the changing aspects of the world around you. Rituals become part of your routine, whether it's a simple prayer before breakfast or a stroll in the park after work to give thanks for the plants and trees. Because of this, you might make other changes closer to home. For example, perhaps you will want to set up a sacred space in your home that you can use to meditate and perform spells and rituals. You might want to introduce magical elements in every room, to remind you of what's important and the path you're following, or perhaps you'll build up a spiritual library of books and journals. Because of their love of nature and the earth, many Wiccans like to grow things, and cultivate fruit and vegetable gardens or allotments. It's up to you how you incorporate your beliefs, and it's important to do what feels right for you.

Preparing for Magical Work

Magic can happen anywhere. As any Wiccan will tell you, it's in every tree and plant, and around every corner; it's in the busy city streets and in those quieter spots. Magic is energy, so it exists in everything. It's about how you think and feel. All this means that you can perform a ritual almost anywhere, using your mind, a symbolic gesture or action, and a few choice words. You can't always prepare yourself for magical work, depending on your circumstances. But as a Wiccan you'll already be developing self-awareness, measuring your thoughts and feelings, and working with the energy around you. So cleansing your body, mind, and spirit should be part of your routine.

CLEANSING RITUALS

When working with any kind of energy, it's important to perform a cleansing ritual on yourself. This eliminates any negative energy in your aura, the energy field around the body. Our energy fields are constantly interfered with and unbalanced by other people, daily events, and even our own negative thoughts. This negative energy drains our vitality and it's important to cleanse our aura and stay balanced. Cleansing rituals will also clear your mind, helping with focus and clarity, and making it easier for you to become attuned to your spiritual energy.

CLEANSING ENERGY

Place a handful of freshly chopped sage leaves into a bowl of hot water. As the vapor rises, inhale deeply and use your hand to waft it around your body. Imagine the aromatic steam cleansing your aura from top to toe. Try to visualize white light surrounding your body and clearing away any negative energy.

WICCAN WISDOM

Some online specialist stores sell smudge sticks. These are used by Native Americans in rituals to cleanse the aura. Made up of a number of different herbs, including sage and sweet grass, they can be burned and passed around the body.

WICCAN WISDOM

Invest in a circular mat that you can
use to mark the area. This will also
help you to visualize the circle clearly.

THE CIRCLE

Before sacred rituals or spell–work, many Wiccans cast a circle.
The circle has been used throughout history and has ancient
origins. The earliest forms of the magic circle have been found
in ancient Babylonian magic, and there are also records of its
use during the Middle Ages and Renaissance.

The circle is important because it creates a space where energy
can be increased, and where the practitioner is protected. The
circle can be a physical one marked out with stones, crystals, or
candles, or it can be imaginary, formed through visualization and
by asking the spirits to bless the space.

CIRCLE RITUAL

*Stand in the area that you would like to work in. Take
a deep breath and, as you breathe out, sweep your
arms up and outward in a circular motion. Imagine a
ray of white light shooting from your fingertips to
form a circle that surrounds you. Say "Spirits of the
north, south, east, and west, help to keep my circle
blessed. Protect and nurture within this space, to
make this my most sacred place. So mote it be!"*

Magical Tools

You can use almost anything in a ritual or spell, but there are certain tools that are sacred and will enhance your magical request. These traditional objects feature in folklore, and learning about them will give you an insight into how and why magic works. The tools listed are some of the most common magical items; however, you don't need to work with them all. Read through and decide what feels right for you at the present moment.

The Wand

This is probably one of the first things that springs to mind when you think of the magical arts. Wands are powerful tools that are used to focus energy by amplifying and directing the intention. A wand can be used to charge an amulet or stone simply by pointing the wand at the object to be charged while visualizing your aims and casting a spell. The Celts made their wands from the wood of specific trees to enhance their power. For example, the rowan or mountain ash was known as the "witches tree," so its wood was a popular choice, as was that of the willow, which was associated with divination. Today, a wand can be made out of almost anything, as long as it's fairly uniform in shape and easy to handle. Even a simple twig from your garden can work well as a wand, as it will connect to your energy and power. Wands can also be decorated with magical symbols, jewels, and crystals to amplify their power and effectiveness.

Wand Ritual

Licorice is used in spells for power and strength, which, strange as it may seem, makes it an excellent choice for a temporary wand. On a piece of paper, write down your aim summed up in a word, for example "love," "health," "strength." Take a licorice stick in both hands and imagine a stream of light flowing through you, traveling down your arms and through your hands into the stick. Say "With light and love in all I do, my aim complete, my wish come true!" Imagine a bolt of light shooting from the stick into the paper where you have written your request.

THE CAULDRON

Traditionally a symbol of the womb, the cauldron is associated with wisdom, death, and rebirth, and is linked to the Greek triple goddess Hecate and the Celtic goddess of the underworld, Cerridwen. Usually made from cast iron with three legs, cauldrons are often displayed on altars and used to burn herbs and incense. They can also be used to create magical brews and elixirs.

CAULDRON RITUAL

If you're searching for answers, fill a cauldron or pot with warm water and add a few drops of lavender essential oil. Close your eyes and ask any question, then open them slightly with your eyelids relaxed and gaze into the cauldron's depths. You may see shapes or shadows that remind you of letters or words; you may even see a pattern or image developing in your mind. Let these thoughts come and go, and when you're ready, make a note of them. They may prove to be useful insights into the future.

THE BROOMSTICK

Our pagan ancestors used the broomstick in rituals for cleansing and also bonding. During many festivals, and especially at midsummer, the broomstick would be laid on the ground and young couples wishing to pledge their love and commitment would jump over it together. Broomsticks were also used to seal the circle when performing spells, and in cleansing rituals to sweep away the past or anything no longer needed. Tales tell of witches using them to fly. In reality, they were used as tools to promote astral travel, with various concoctions rubbed into the broom to encourage flying dreams and hallucinations. Today, the broom is a useful tool for cleansing and to clear the path for something new.

BROOMSTICK RITUAL

Soak your broom or a sweeping brush in hot water mixed with a few drops of basil and sage essential oils. Leave the broom to dry and then use it to sweep the path, step, or entrance into your home. This will trigger positive energy and encourage the flow of money into your home.

THE ATHAME

An athame is a magical knife used in Wiccan rituals and ceremonies to direct power. It combines the uses of the wand and the sword, helping to cast a circle and project energy. Some Wiccans choose to decorate their athame by engraving it with symbols, words, or runes. Traditionally, witches would use an athame with a white hilt for general magic and one with a black hilt for casting circles and protection. Today, it's common to use one athame for everything, including cooking. This might sound odd, but cooking a lovely meal is often likened to conjuring a spell as it uses the same principles of intention and ritual. As with almost all magical items, your athame will grow in power as you use and handle it.

ATHAME RITUAL

Invest in an interesting knife that you can use for your magical work. Anoint the hilt with a mixture of lavender and rosemary essential oils. Wrap in black silk and leave it in the light of a full moon to charge it with power.

THE CHALICE

This ornate goblet is often used in magical rites and rituals to represent the element water. The chalice can be made from many materials, including gold, silver, brass, and crystal. During a ceremony, the chalice will be filled with water or wine, which is then drunk in worship or as part of a spell. Many Wiccans keep a chalice on their altar as a representation of this element.

CHALICE RITUAL

Keep a special glass or goblet as a chalice for rituals and spell work. To cleanse the chalice, place a piece of amethyst in it, cover with salted water, and leave overnight. In the morning, remove the crystal and rinse the chalice well, then fill with sparkling water and a squeeze of lemon juice. Sip whilst visualizing your third–eye chakra (in the center of your forehead) opening up. This ritual promotes psychic awareness.

THE BELL

In ancient times, our ancestors would ring a "passing bell" when someone was on the brink of death, to drive away evil spirits. The idea that the bell is associated with protection and cleansing is common throughout mythology and in pagan lore. Many Wiccans use bells in their rituals, or to cleanse an area in their home. The act of ringing the bell loudly is enough to clear the space of any negative energy. Some Wiccans choose to hang a bell outside their front door to guard their home. Bells can also be used in rituals and are rung to mark the beginning or end of a spell.

BELL RITUAL

To create a harmonious atmosphere, burn some bergamot and orange essential oils. Take a drop of sunflower oil, which is associated with joy, and massage it into your bell. Then spend a few minutes ringing the bell, whilst moving around your home and chanting "Happiness is mine from this moment in time."

THE MORTAR AND PESTLE

An essential tool for anyone following the craft, the mortar and pestle will help you to grind herbs and spices for spells. This is an important part of the magical process, because you can put your energy and intention into the ingredients as you grind.

MORTAR AND PESTLE RITUAL

Grind a pinch of sea salt using your mortar and pestle. As you do so, visualize a lightning bolt of energy coming from the sky straight into the salt and infusing it with power. Grind until the salt is fine and powdery, then sprinkle it into your bathwater for protection and strength.

Signs and Symbols

In the Wiccan tradition, there are a number of signs and symbols that appear frequently and are used in magical practice, or to represent elements and ideas. These symbols help us to tap into the energy associated with the element or idea. Part of the Wiccan tradition involves reading and understanding signs, particularly those that occur naturally in the environment. As you develop your intuition, you'll instinctively recognize signs and symbols and what they mean to you. Below are some of the best-known Wiccan symbols.

THE PENTAGRAM

A popular pagan symbol, often used for protection, the pentagram is a five-pointed star inside a circle. Each point represents an element—earth, air, fire, water, and spirit. Wiccans often wear a pentagram to show that they're connected to the elements and the cycles of life. This ancient symbol has been linked to many great civilizations, and represents power, strength, and spiritual development.

PENTACLE

Many covens customize the symbol of the pentagram into a pentacle, to represent their focus and specific message. A pentacle looks like a pentagram, but it is not written down. It's usually formed out of clay or wax, or fashioned into jewelry that can be worn as a form of protection.

PENTAGRAM POWER

To protect your home and promote positive energy in your life, gather some brick dust from the walls by brushing them with a paintbrush. Sprinkle the dust in the shape of a pentagram beneath a floor mat near the entrance, or outside your back door.

PENTACLE SPELL

Take a black candle for protection and, with a pin, carve a pentacle into the wax. Rub a little lavender essential oil into the pentacle whilst visualizing a circle of white light surrounding you and those you love. Light the candle and let it burn down, whilst continuing to picture the circle of light.

THE GODDESS

The symbol of the goddess, which looks like the three phases of the moon connected, representing the mother, maiden, and crone (the three stages of the goddess), is important to Wiccans. The goddess is the nurturing female element, Mother Earth, who supports us in all things. She's an archetype that appears in mythology around the world, and is used to tap into different elements of magic. Wiccans learn to work with and embrace her energy, and often wear this symbol as a way of connecting to her power and also drawing down the power of the moon.

GODDESS MOON RITUAL

Stand in the light of the full moon and, with a stick draw the symbol of the goddess in the earth at your feet. Place a piece of moonstone in the center of the symbol and ask the moon to bless you with her power and grace.

THE HORNED GOD

This is the symbol of divine male energy. The horned god is the male counterpart of the goddess. He's the lord of the hunt and is often linked to the wild woods. He is born during the winter solstice, and unites with the goddess only to die and be reborn again as the seasons move on. He represents the cycles of life and death, and appears in mythologies around the world. His symbol is a circle with a crescent moon on top.

HORNED GOD CHARM

If you're looking for inspiration and you'd like to stimulate your creative energy, invest in a piece of jewelry bearing the symbol of the horned god. Alternatively, draw the symbol on a piece of paper, and place it beneath your pillow at night. Ask the god to speak to you through your dreams.

THE TRIQUETRA

A Celtic symbol, often used as a grave-marker or on plaques, the triquetra represents ideas that come in threes. It is often associated with the mother, maiden, and crone aspects of the triple goddess, and it can also refer to the past, present, and future. A popular Wiccan symbol, it's often worn as a piece of jewelry.

THE WHEEL OF THE YEAR

Often called the sun symbol, the wheel of the year represents the eight sabbats (festivals) celebrated by Wiccans throughout the year. Each section of the wheel relates to a particular festival, and the wheel itself is a symbol of the continuing cycle of life, and how we move through each season.

TRIANGLE CHARM

The triquetra is triangular, and you can use its power to attract good fortune. Write down your wish for the future in a sentence, and draw a triangle next to it. Start placing the words from your sentence inside the triangle. Fold the paper into a triangular parcel, secure it with string, and leave it on a window ledge in the light of the moon.

WHEEL RITUAL

Place a white candle in a dish on top of the Wheel of Fortune tarot card (for more on tarot, see page 135). Light the candle and give thanks for the changing seasons and the wheel of the year. Remember that as the wheel turns, it brings change and evolution. See yourself riding a giant Ferris wheel, rising to the top, and experiencing the joy of movement and energy, and then riding to the bottom again.

THE TRISKELE

Another Celtic symbol, the triskele looks like three legs running and is associated with movement and the cycles of life. The three legs represent three different aspects—mind, body, and spirit—and some scholars believe that they're linked to the three worlds—the otherworld, the mortal world, and the celestial world. Because of this, the symbol is often thought to represent personal growth and development.

ANKH RITUAL

Embrace life and give thanks by performing this easy ritual first thing in the morning. Throw the drapes back and welcome the gift of the sun. Stand with your feet together and your arms outstretched at shoulder height, making the shape of the ankh. Look upward and bring your arms together above your head, then sweep them apart in a circular motion, returning them to your sides when you've finished. Repeat three times, whilst (if necessary) imagining that you're bathed in sunlight.

TRISKELE SPELL

If you want to get things moving in a particular area of your life, draw the triskele in the center of a piece of paper. Trace over the shape nine times, whilst chanting "I move forward with grace, let action take place."

THE EYE OF HORUS

Often referred to as the all–seeing eye, this powerful Egyptian symbol is associated with protection and healing, and is a popular choice for amulets and charms. It was associated with a number of deities, including Bast, Hathor, Ra, and Wadjet. Fashioned out of gold, silver, lapis lazuli, or carnelian, it was traditionally worn for protection.

THE ANKH

This ancient Egyptian symbol of eternal life is often used in spells or worn as a charm. Some scholars believe that it evolved from a glyph for magical protection; others think it represents male and female energy. Associated with many of the gods and widely used in decoration, the ankh is also linked to wisdom.

SACRED EYE AMULET

Create your own amulet for strength and protection. Trace the shape of an eye in permanent blue or black marker pen onto a stone. Bury it in the ground and leave it overnight to absorb the earth's energy. Remove and keep it with you, or place it beneath your pillow at night.

The Flow of Synchronicity

As you learn more about the Wiccan path and your intuition grows, you'll start to notice the small coincidences in your life that really make a difference: the times when things seem to fall into place, or when you receive a sign that makes you stop and think or resonates with how you've been feeling. Often we're unaware of these events because we go through life with our heads down and a blinkered view of the world. This is because other things take over: we're so absorbed in our own problems and worries that it's easy to miss or shrug off these coincidences. But as you become more self-aware, and aware of your environment, you'll recognize these signs and symbols and understand their power. You'll feel a whirl of energy pulling you in a certain direction and you'll embrace it.

This magical flow of events, when something happens at just the right time and you connect with it on a deeper level, is called synchronicity. For example, perhaps you've been thinking of exploring the healing power of crystals but don't know where to start. On your usual trip into work you see something glinting by the road. As you get closer, you realize it's a leaflet advertising a new book on crystal power. You decide to follow your intuition and head to a bookstore on your lunch break to buy the book. When you get there, not only do you find the book, but also, as you're paying, you notice a small poster advertising a one-day workshop on the healing power of stones and crystals. You attend the workshop and start chatting to the instructor, who invites you to a crystal healing session, where you meet like-minded people and develop your skills. Because you were self-aware and going with the flow of synchronicity, your initial dream became a reality. But if you hadn't stopped to pick up the leaflet, you might never have entered the bookstore, seen the poster, or attended that first influential workshop.

Opening up to the synchronicity in your life feels good. This is because you're working with your higher self and getting to know what's important to you. You're discovering your life path and engaging your intuition to find the answers and seek a way forward. This doesn't mean that you'll see signs and symbols all the time, but it does mean that you'll recognize the right ones when they appear. You'll identify that feeling of excitement and a tug in your solar plexus (just above your belly button), and you'll instinctively know that you must pay attention and take action. Opposite are some tips that will help you to open up to the flow of synchronicity in your life.

SYNCHRONICITY IN ACTION

Spend ten minutes every day in quiet contemplation. Focus on your breathing and let thoughts come and go, as if you were watching a movie.

Citrine is an excellent stone for opening your mind and heart to new adventures. Keep a piece in your pocket at all times.

Listen to what others tell you. Those close to us often notice things that we don't.

Engage all your senses as you go about your daily routine: see, hear, touch, taste, and smell your environment.

Pay attention to your feelings and where they appear in your body. A strong tingling sensation just above your belly button could be your intuition trying to tell you something. Similarly, a warm feeling in your chest area could indicate that something positive is coming.

Ask for a sign every day that you are on the right path.

Connect to your higher self by activating your crown chakra: imagine a white flower opening up in the center of your scalp.

CHAPTER 2

SPELLS, RITUALS, AND CHARMS

Understanding Spells

What is a spell and how does it work? This is a question often asked by those exploring witchcraft. On the surface, a spell appears to be a carefully selected set of words put together in a specific way to generate great magical power, and create positive change. Although there is some truth in the power of words and the way we connect them, the real power behind any spell is the intention. In other words, what do you hope to gain from the spell? What is your desired outcome? A spell is just a way of making your intention obvious to the universe, and of allowing you to put some energy behind it. For example, when you make a wish and blow out the candles on a birthday cake, you're really performing a simple spell. You have an intention in mind and you follow this through by doing something active (blowing out the candles). The action, also known as a ritual, cements your commitment and focus.

Casting a Spell

For a spell to work, you need three things: intention, action, and belief, in that order.

Intention
Before you plan any spell, ask yourself why you are doing it. Is it through genuine need and a desire to make things better? Or is it because you think a spell is a shortcut to what you have in mind? Life is difficult, and you might think using magic is an easy route to happiness, but nothing is set in stone. Sometimes we're set challenges for a reason, and when things don't go our way it's not because the magic hasn't worked; it's because something else is coming, something that's better for us at that time. So although spells can and do work, they're not always the answer. Consider whether there's another way to get what you want before attempting a spell.

It's important to remember that although a spell might attract a set of opportunities, it's up to you to grab them and take physical action. Always look out for signs and openings that help to further your cause. Magic works in mysterious ways; sometimes it creates the perfect set of circumstances to help you get what you want, but it still requires you to take a leap of faith.

Belief

This is the cherry on the cake. Once you've decided what you want and have performed your ritual, you need to believe that it's actually happening for you. Picture your desired outcome. Imagine it as an image surrounded by golden light, then see it flying up into the universe like a balloon. Know that it is in safe hands, and that you've set magical powers in motion to make it work for you. Try not to worry about the outcome or cling desperately to it. The more you do that, the more you restrict the flow of energy around you. For a spell to work you must be open to the universe, connected to the energy of the earth, and able to read subtle signs and synchronicities. You can't do this if you're riddled with fear, doubt, or anxiety. So let your wish fly away, relax, and be happy in the knowledge that everything is working out perfectly for you.

Action

Once you're sure of your intention, you need to think of an action or ritual to represent it. A ritual can be elaborate or easy, depending on your aim and how you feel. It can be as simple as saying a rhyme or chant, lighting a candle, or planting a seed in a pot, as long as it matches your intention and indicates your commitment to the spell. You can include ingredients that resonate with your desire, or those that are related to a particular planet or energy. For example, apples are often associated with love and with Venus (the goddess as well as the planet), so they're the perfect choice for love spells. If you're looking for new love, you might plant some apple seeds in a pot whilst making a wish for love to grow. If you're hoping to cement an existing relationship, you might cut an apple in half, drizzle it with honey (also associated with love), and give it to your other half, whilst wishing for your love to flourish. Each of these rituals matches the aim and, if performed with energy and belief, will be effective.

External and Internal Spells

Spells work on two levels. They can either affect your external circumstances, such as a candle spell to attract good luck into your life, or they can affect how you feel in yourself, like a bath soak for health and beauty. So when you're deciding what type of spell you need, start by thinking about the overall effect. Do you want to change how you think and feel, or do you want to change factors outside of yourself?

HOW TO CREATE A RITUAL

Once you have decided on the type of spell and your desired outcome, you will have a clearer idea about the kind of ritual you'd like to use. For example, if you need to take swift action to call in your debts, you might work with the element fire and use some candle magic. This is external, works quickly, and produces action and movement. But if you want to heal a broken heart—an

internal problem—you might choose water magic and prepare a soothing elixir to drink. A spell to gain a promotion at work might require a mix of both types of magic, because for success at work you must both feel confident and let others see how fantastic you are. So you could work with fire by burning some oil and herbs and adding them to your bathwater.

It's also worth considering the type of change you're trying to create, and whether it's for a short-term goal or something more long-term. If you're trying to manifest something big, you might need a longer, more complex ritual with lots of ingredients.

Ritual checklist
This checklist should give you a clear idea of the type of spell that will work, and will help you put together a successful ritual.

1) Do I want to change how I think and feel with this spell?
2) Do I want to change how others see me?
3) Do I want to change outside circumstances?
4) Do I want swift action?
5) Am I looking to manifest a small change?
6) Am I looking to manifest a big change?

The X Factor: Adding Extra Power

Once you have your intention and you've decided on the type of spell and ritual to support it, you're almost there. But there's one special ingredient you need to add for success, and that's the X factor—X for extra power. Think of it as like firing an arrow: you home in on your target, fit the arrow to the bow, then pull back and release. This final action sets things in motion. It's a burst of energy as you send the arrow on its way. Similarly, when you create a spell, you need to inject some of your personal energy into the proceedings. The easiest way to do this is to believe that the outcome has already come true.

TRY THIS

Visualize the outcome of the spell clearly in your mind and imagine how you'll feel when it happens. Run through all the emotions and really believe that your wish has been fulfilled. As you perform the ritual, hold an image in your mind of the desired result. Draw your attention to your heart chakra, in the middle of your chest. How does it feel? You may notice a warm, tingling sensation that spreads through your body. Imagine pouring this magical energy into the spell.

WICCAN WISDOM

Imagine a dart of light shooting from your heart chakra out into the universe as you recite your spell. This flame of light enhances your message and gives it extra power.

CHARMS AND AMULETS

If you wish to effect change over a long period of time—for example, you want to perform a protection spell that will last far into the future—you might want to create a charm or amulet. These are items that are charged with an intention, usually by performing a ritual, and then kept as a magical tool to create the desired effect. Many magical practitioners use crystals and stones because they naturally transmit and conduct energy, but anything—whether jewelry or another object—can be a charm or amulet, as long as it has significance to the wearer and is charged correctly.

HOW TO CHARGE A CHARM

The best way to charge a charm is to imagine that you're pouring your intention into it. Start by creating the right atmosphere, perhaps by lighting a candle or burning some oil. Create a sacred space and place your charm in the center. If you're working with a crystal or stone, always soak it overnight in salty water to cleanse it of any negative energy or residue from being handled previously. Imagine a ball of light in the center of your forehead, the area known as the third-eye chakra. Hold your intention in your mind, and picture a thread of light spinning from your third eye into the charm. You might want to say a few words at this point, such as "I charge this charm with light and love. So mote it be!" Keep the charm somewhere safe, like a velvet charm bag, or wrapped in black silk.

REMEMBER!

Charms should be recharged every few months to maintain their power.

Starter Spells

To get you started, here are some easy spells covering a variety of areas. There is also a list of ingredients associated with each area, so that you can experiment and create your own spells.

PROTECTION SPELLS

Ingredients for protection spells
Bamboo, blackberry, blueberry, broccoli, cactus, chili powder, garlic, lemon, mango, mustard, onion, pepper, radish, rosemary, rue, salt, sunflower seeds, vinegar

Colors
Black, red, white

BAMBOO STAFF

Bamboo is a wonderful plant that takes very little effort to maintain and is linked to power and protection.

***You will need**: A pin, a bamboo stick, sunflower oil, a vase, and water*

Using the pin, carve your initials into the stem of the bamboo. Massage a drop of sunflower oil into the bamboo. Place in a vase with some water and say "Straight and tall, strong and true, like the mighty bamboo, I'm protected and nurtured in all that I do." Keep the vase in a prominent place and repeat the chant every day.

PELE'S CIRCLE OF FIRE

Pele is the Hawaiian goddess of fire and volcanoes. Powerful and feisty, she can help you to remain strong, and protect you in times of trouble.

***You will need**: A red candle*

Light the candle and watch as the flame grows in size and length. Close your eyes and imagine a flame in your solar plexus, just above your belly button. See it grow and expand until it fills your stomach with warmth. Now imagine a protective circle of fire surrounding you. Say "Pele, with your circle of fire, give me the strength that I desire." Let the candle burn down as you hold the image of the circle of fire in your mind.

HEALTH SPELLS

Ingredients for health spells
Almond, apple, cucumber, honey, lemon, lettuce, mango, melon, olive, orange, parsley, peppermint, sage, thyme, tomato

Colors
Blue, green, pink, white, yellow

MANGO MAGIC

Mango is a tasty fruit with a strong, empowering energy that will give your vitality a boost.

***You will need**: A mango, a knife, orange juice*

Cut out a section of mango to eat. Remove the skin and eat the flesh. Carve the word "strength" into the piece of skin and leave it to dry on the windowsill (it should take about a week). When it's dry, massage a splash of orange juice into the skin whilst picturing yourself glowing with health and vitality. Place the dried skin beneath your pillow for a week.

FLOWER FAIRY SPELL

Tap into some fairy magic and use the vibrant power of flowers for healing.

***You will need**: A handful of yellow flowers such as daffodils or roses, a blue vase and some water, a quartz crystal*

Yellow flowers are associated with fairy spirits and positive energy, whilst blue is the color of healing. Collect the flowers and display them in the vase with some water. Place a piece of quartz in front of the vase. If the spell is for you, sit for a few minutes in front of the flowers and make a wish for healing. If it's to heal someone else, place their photograph in front of the flowers and make a wish for their recovery. Also make a gift of the flowers to the sick person.

LOVE SPELLS

Ingredients for love spells
Almond, apple, avocado, banana, basil, catnip, cheese, cherry, chestnut, cream, ginger, hazelnut, milk, mint, orange, raspberry, strawberry, tomato, vanilla

Colors
Gold, pink, red, white

APPLE SEED SPELL

Apples are associated with the Greek goddess of love and beauty, Aphrodite (the Roman Venus), and can be used to help you find a soul mate.

You will need*: A piece of paper, a pen, an apple*

On the paper, write down your wish for love. If you're looking for a soul mate, for example, write down what you hope this person would be like. Cut the apple in half and scoop out the seeds. Find an oak tree and sit beneath its branches. Say your love request out loud, then find a spot of earth and bury the seeds and the paper together.

GINGER LOVE CHARM

Ginger root will spice up a relationship and can get things moving if you're looking for romantic action.

You will need*: ginger root (either a piece that looks like two stuck together, or two separate pieces), some red string or cotton*

Tie the string around the ginger root three times. If you have two pieces of root, tie them securely together. Say "As two become one, our bonds grow strong. True love is mine, from this moment in time." Keep the root with you as a charm to increase the flow of love into your life.

MONEY SPELLS

Ingredients for money spells
Barley, basil, bay leaves, beans, cinnamon, clove, fig, frankincense, grape, mint, oats, parsley, pea, rice, sesame seeds

Colors
Gold, green, yellow

FINANCIAL FIRE SPELL

This spell combines the powerful effects of fire magic with some money-making herbs.

You will need: *dried mint, frankincense resin, a fireproof bowl, a dried bay leaf, a candle or lighter*

Place the mint and frankincense into the bowl. On the bay leaf, write the word "money." Pass the leaf through a flame so that it starts to burn, and drop it into the bowl. Say "I raise this magical energy to bring financial boon to me. The money that I need today, is now securely on its way!" When the contents of the bowl have finished burning, scatter the ashes outside in the light of a waxing moon.

BASIL PURSE CHARM

Basil is known as the money herb, because its large green leaves resemble notes. Use its energy to attract more cash.

You will need: *a blank check, fresh basil leaves, a wallet or purse*

Write on the check the amount of money you'd like to attract into your life. Be positive and realistic about this amount. Fold a couple basil leaves into the check and place it in your wallet or purse. As you do this, picture your bank account and imagine the amount of money increasing until you have the sum you desire.

SUCCESS SPELLS

Ingredients for success spells

Apple, bergamot, cardamom, cheese, cinnamon, fig, frankincense, honey, juniper, lemon, orange, pumpkin, strawberry, sunflower seeds

Colors

Gold, orange, red, yellow

MIDAS TOUCH SPELL

Affirmations can be powerful magical tools. This spell combines the power of words with visualization to help you succeed.

You will need: *bergamot essential oil, an oil burner*

Find a quiet spot and burn the bergamot oil. Take a few deep breaths and clear your mind. Picture yourself standing on a path that leads to your destination, signposted "success." Repeat in your head the affirmation "Everything I touch turns to gold." See yourself walking toward your destination. Imagine that with each step the path changes from gray to sparkling gold, and that everything around you begins to turn to gold. Keep repeating the affirmation, and when you're ready, open your eyes. Every morning, reinforce the magic of these words by repeating them in front of a mirror.

VICTORY TIPPLE

Success is often influenced by how we feel on the inside. This spell works on your confidence to ensure victory.

You will need: *a lemon tea bag, hot water, honey, ground cinnamon*

Steep the tea bag in hot water for a few minutes and remove. Add a spoonful of honey and a sprinkling of cinnamon to the water. Stir whilst picturing yourself as super-successful. Before you drink, say "I radiate confidence and finesse. Everything I do is a great success!" Sip the magical brew whilst picturing yourself achieving your goals.

BEAUTY SPELLS

Ingredients for beauty spells
Allspice, anise, banana, carob, chocolate, geranium, honey, lavender, lemon, milk, olives and olive oil, pine nuts, rose, rosemary, sunflower seeds and sunflower oil, vanilla

Colors
Gold, pink, purple, red, silver, white

OSHUN BATH SOAK

Oshun is the Yoruban goddess of love and beauty. Use her power to let your inner beauty shine through.

You will need: *1 cup (250ml) milk, a pan, 1 tbsp (15 ml) honey, a pinch of grated nutmeg, a mug*

Gently heat the milk in the pan until it's warm but not boiling. Add the honey, and stir whilst picturing yourself looking like a goddess. Add the nutmeg to the mixture and pour into the mug. Add to running bathwater and soak whilst repeating the affirmation "I let my inner goddess shine."

ROSEMARY ELIXIR

Rosemary is a powerful herb that enhances a woman's natural charms.

You will need: *Fresh rosemary, hot water, a bowl, geranium essential oil*

Steep a handful of rosemary in a bowl of hot water for 10–15 minutes. Add a couple drops of geranium essential oil, bend over the bowl, and inhale deeply for five minutes. As you do this, repeat the following chant either out loud or in your mind: "I am strong and beautiful. I radiate power."

SPELLS FOR GOOD FORTUNE

Ingredients for good fortune spells
Basil, beans, cinnamon, coconut, frankincense, hazelnut, lemon, noodles, nutmeg, orange, pasta, sunflower seeds and sunflower oil

Colors
Gold, green, orange, yellow

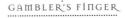

GAMBLER'S FINGER

Spices bring action and movement, and in magical circles nutmeg is known as the gambler's charm.

***You will need**: Grated nutmeg, a drop of sunflower oil, a saucer*

In a saucer, stir together a drop of sunflower oil, which promotes success, and a pinch of the gambler's charm, nutmeg, with your finger. Massage into the palms of both hands whilst making a wish for good luck. Rinse off with warm water.

LADY LUCK FLOOR WASH

This floor wash will encourage good fortune into your home or workplace.

***You will need**: A handful of fresh basil leaves, a cup, boiling water, hot soapy water, a bucket, the juice of half a lemon, frankincense essential oil*

Steep the basil leaves in a cup of boiling water for five minutes. Strain the liquid into a bucket of hot soapy water with the lemon juice and five drops of frankincense essential oil. Use as a floor wash on your front and back step or entrance hall. As you mop, imagine you're painting the floor and entrance bright gold.

WISH SPELLS

Ingredients for wish spells
Apples, bananas, carob, cheese, chestnuts, chocolate, corn, hazelnuts, nutmeg, sugar, water, red or white wine

Colors
Gold, purple, silver, white

SUGAR AND SPICE

Sugar is sweet and attracts good things. Combine its energy with spice to get things moving in your life.

***You will need**: A white candle, 1 tsp (5 ml) sugar, 1 tsp (5 ml) mixed spice*

Light the candle and sprinkle the sugar in a circle around it whilst saying "I draw my wish to me, as it should be." Sprinkle the mixed spice in a circle on top of the sugar, saying "Powerful action that is fast, my wish comes true at last!" Let the candle burn down, then scatter the sugar and spice outside whilst repeating the chants.

WATER MAGIC

Flowing water of any kind can help to carry your wish to the universe, where it will be granted.

***You will need**: a pen and paper, a flower of any kind*

Write down your wish on the paper, and use it to wrap the flower. Find a stream or river and spend a few moments there thinking about your wish. Throw the flower and paper into the flowing water and say "As the water flows, so my wish grows."

PSYCHIC AWARENESS SPELLS

Ingredients for psychic awareness spells
Bay leaves, celery, cucumber, dandelion, fish (all types), lavender, lettuce, mint, mushrooms, thyme

Colors
Indigo, purple, silver, white

PSYCHIC BREW

This soothing tea will help to open your mind and trigger your sixth sense.

***You will need**: a handful of lettuce leaves, fresh mint, a sprig of thyme, a sprig of lavender, a pan, boiling water, a teapot, a cup*

Place all the ingredients in a pan with boiling water. Let it simmer for 10–15 minutes, stirring occasionally. Strain the liquid into a teapot and pour out a cup. As you sip, imagine a thread of light stretching from the middle of your scalp up into the sky. This cord connects you to the universe and the universal subconscious. Drink the tea before bed to promote prophetic dreams.

AMETHYST EYE OPENER

This spell uses the energy of amethyst to stimulate the third eye chakra, in the middle of the forehead.

***You will need**: a flannel, warm water, lavender essential oil, a piece of amethyst*

Soak the flannel in warm water and add a couple drops of lavender essential oil. Wrap the amethyst in the flannel and hold it in the middle of your forehead. Close your eyes and breathe deeply. Imagine a purple flower located in your third eye chakra, and see it slowly opening its petals until they're fully extended. In the center of the flower is a ball of purple light. Imagine it spreading behind your eyes and filling your head. Make a note of any thoughts or images that come to you, as these might be psychic insights.

HERBAL MAGIC

The Power of Nature

As you follow the Wiccan path, you'll begin to work with the natural energy that surrounds you. You'll feel more connected to the earth, and you'll discover that Mother Nature provides everything you could possibly need to live a happy, harmonious existence. Those who are naturally drawn to herbal magic have an affinity with nature. They understand the power of plants, herbs, and flowers, and their place in the world. Many centuries ago, our ancestors used these gifts in healing spells and to manifest the things they needed. Herbs were added to food, not just because they tasted good, but because they had some benefit. Witches and wise women understood that every ingredient had a specific energy that could be used. They worked with nature, tapping into this energy and directing it to bring about positive change.

Today we use herbal magic in spells and rituals to ensure success. A wealth of material is available that explains the use of herbs, how to grow them, and what they're good for. It's a fascinating subject, and you may wish to delve further and experiment. Most Wiccans have some knowledge of herb lore. They can identify plants and herbs and often grow their own to use in spells. Urban witches living in large cities might not have access to a plot of land where they can create their own herb garden, but through the power of the Internet they can obtain dried herbs from magical suppliers. So if you're drawn to this kind of magic, there's always a way to explore and learn more.

Each season would bring its own blessings, unique gifts from the earth. Seeds were sown during the spring, and plants were harvested during those late summer months. Some herbs flourished all year round while others had a particular time when they grew in strength and potency. For example, mint tends to thrive during September and October, while parsley, thyme, and sage do well all year round. Rosemary on the other hand, prefers warmer climates. Our ancestors understood this. They gleaned their knowledge not from books or scientific experiments but through watching and waiting. Learning to understand the ebb and flow of nature and passing on what they'd learned by word of mouth. They believed in the power of the goddess, likening the earth to her womb and the plants, flowers, and herbs to her offspring. They worshipped this feminine life–giving power by lighting fires and using them in ceremonial rituals to ensure a good harvest.

The Celts, in particular, would dance around their fires, sometimes leaping over them with cattle to secure a prosperous outcome and fertile land. It was common place to leave offerings of herbs and flowers on fields that had been harvested, or to scatter seeds around trees. Deities were petitioned, usually earth goddesses or those linked to the spark of new life, like the Celtic Goddess Áine, and the Green Man was also celebrated for his place in protecting the surroundings. The triple goddess, who represents the three phases of womanhood, from maiden to mother and then crone, was also honored. In some parts of the UK, particularly the highlands of Scotland, farmers would gather the last sheaf and turn it into a young maiden, which they likened to the maiden aspect of the triple goddess. This was thought to represent a good harvest; but if the harvest had been bad, they would turn it into an old hag, which symbolized the crone aspect and the often unforgiving and cruel side of nature.

Traditions were born and rituals created that would tap into the energy of the earth, because the ancients respected the land. They wanted not only to help it flourish, but also to give thanks for the crops and gifts that it provided. They realized that they couldn't control nature, but they could learn to work with it. Much can be learned from the old ways. Even if you don't feel a calling for this type of magic, you'll understand the important role that it plays in the Wiccan path.

Working with Herbs

Begin with something you know about. If you regularly use herbs in your cooking, start with those. Learn about their medicinal and magical uses. What are their associations, and how can you combine them in spells?

Invest in a range of tools to help you work with fresh herbs. For example, you might want to have a special basket that you use for drying the herbs you harvest. It's also a good idea to invest in a special knife for cutting herbs, and a mortar and pestle so that you can grind them.

- Keep your magical tools separate from your cooking utensils. Cleanse them regularly using salty water, and use them only when preparing ingredients for spells and rituals.

- Create your own miniature herb garden on a window ledge with pots of the most popular and commonly used herbs. Go for things that are easy to look after, such as sage, thyme, basil, and rosemary.

- Bring the outside in and fill your house with flowers and plants. This will strengthen your connection to nature, and also promote the flow of positive energy through your home.

- If you have a yard, create your own herb garden outside. Decide which herbs you want to grow, and the best place to grow them. Some herbs like dark, dry spaces, and others prefer sunlight and room to breathe, so it's worth looking into this for the best chance of success in the conditions you can provide.

- In folklore, herbs like lavender and rosemary were thought to attract fairy spirits, and some people believed that wherever rosemary grew in abundance, there was a strong and magical woman. Get to know the myths and tales associated with each herb to give you an insight into its magical uses.

Most importantly, have fun and experiment. If you feel that two herbs will work well together in a ritua , follow your intuition.

USIПG HERBS

When you use herbs in magic, whether by adding them to food or burning the dried leaves, focus on their energy and imagine it growing and supercharging the spell. Visualize your desired outcome and focus on the emotions associated with it. Give thanks to Mother Earth for supplying you with the ingredients you need, and give something back by planting some seeds, or perhaps leaving an offering of a stone or flower. Get your hands dirty and do some gardening so that you get to grips with the earth and reap the blessings of the environment.

Angelica

Ruled by the sun, angelica is linked to protection. It is used to ward off evil spirits, protect the home, and banish negative energy. Medicinally, the leaves can be used in a tea to relieve coughs and chest infections. A stronger preparation can be made from the root, and used as a tonic for the liver.

AПGELICA RITUAL

To maintain a happy relationship, wrap a piece of angelica root, a pinch of lavender, and a piece of rose quartz in white silk. Leave it beneath the bed to promote love and honesty.

Anise

Associated with the planet Jupiter, anise is used in spells to promote love. It's often used to flavor wedding cakes, to ensure that the couple's relationship will flourish. It is also linked to psychic powers, and a pinch of anise carried in a handkerchief will help you to become more intuitive.

AПISE RITUAL

Burn a small handful of dried anise and inhale the aroma. Close your eyes and let any thoughts or visions come to you. You might also place a pinch of dried anise in a dish with a piece of amber and leave it by your bed for prophetic dreams.

Basil

Ruled by the element fire, this powerful herb is linked to money, success, and love. The large green leaves are thought to represent banknotes, which is why the herb is often used in spells to increase finances. Eating food flavored with basil, such as pesto, is thought to promote and encourage love.

BASIL RITUAL

Place a fresh basil leaf in your wallet. As you do so, imagine the amount of money you'd like to see in your bank account.

Bay leaves

Bay leaves have been used for centuries in folk magic for protection and to make wishes come true. Some people place a bay leaf in each of the four corners of their home to ward off evil. Ruled by the sun, this versatile leaf can be used in lotions, potions, and teas, and can also be burned.

BAY RITUAL

On a dried bay leaf, write down a word to sum up your wish. If you're looking for the perfect partner, for instance, you might write "love," or if you need healing, you might write "health." Light a white candle and pass the leaf through the flame, then drop it into a fireproof bowl. Watch as the leaf burns. If it stays alight for a while, this is thought to be a sign that your wish has been granted.

Chamomile

This masculine herb with lots of medicinal uses is a great addition to any witch's herb garden. A natural sedative, it can also be drunk as a tea to calm the digestive system. In magical terms, it's good for cleansing a sacred space, promoting love and beauty, and ensuring success. It's thought that if you plant chamomile in your garden, you'll attract good fortune.

CHAMOMILE RITUAL

Make a chamomile tea, either by steeping the fresh herb in hot water, or by using a tea bag. Strain the liquid and add a couple drops of lavender essential oil. Let it cool, then use it as a beauty rinse. Splash on your face and pour on wet hair, then rinse off with warm water. Say "My natural beauty shines this day, I am restored in every way."

Chives

This tasty herb, often used in cooking, has always been popular for its ability to repel evil spirits. Because of this, it was often brought into the house and placed near doors and windows. Medicinally, eating chives can help to cleanse the digestive system, although eating too much of this herb has the opposite effect and can cause stomach ache. Ruled by Mars, this powerful herb protects and strengthens the aura.

CHIVES RITUAL

Chop a bundle of fresh chives into roughly 5in (13cm) lengths. Make into two bundles, tie with black cotton or ribbon, and hang them from your front and back doors to keep harmful energy at bay.

Dill

Ruled by the planet Mercury, dill is thought to promote clear and quick thinking, attract love, and ward off evil. The Romans would massage dill-scented oil into their skin before going into battle, and in Germany brides would often include dill in their wedding bouquets to help their love blossom. Today, dill is used in a wide range of spells and can be added to meals to give them a magical punch.

☆
☆
☆ **DILL RITUAL**
☆ ·····································
☆

Add a sprinkling of dill to any fish dish, saying "May the gift of intelligence be mine. My mind is sharp and focused from this moment in time." As you eat the fish, repeat the chant in your head, and imagine a spark of light growing behind your eyes.

Fennel

Another great herb to promote mental alertness, and also used in weight-loss spells, fennel is thought to increase a woman's personal power. Drink as a tea to reduce the appetite, or add to bathwater for an invigorating soak.

☆
☆ **FENNEL RITUAL**
☆ ·····································
☆
☆
☆

Place a handful of fennel seeds into a charm bag. Write your weight-loss goal on a piece of paper, fold it three times, and add it to the charm bag. Finally, visualize yourself slim and healthy, and say "By the power times three, half this size I shall be."

Lavender

An all-round miracle-worker, lavender has long been used to promote sleep and cure headaches, and as a tonic for colds and flu. Our Celtic ancestors threw it on their fires at midsummer as an offering to the deities. Ruled by the element air, lavender can be used in spells for love, peace, purification, and happiness.

☆
☆ **LAVENDER RITUAL**
☆ ·····································
☆
☆
☆ *Make a healing and rejuvenating sachet by tying a*
☆ *bundle of fresh lavender into a piece of cheesecloth.*
☆ *You can increase its power by adding a couple*
drops of lavender essential oil. Tie the sachet at one
end and pop into running bathwater whilst making
a wish for general well-being.

Mint

A sacred herb to druids, mint is ruled by Venus and used in spells for love and healing. Its bright green color and fresh scent also mean that it's used in spells to attract money. Medicinally, mint leaves can be rubbed against the forehead to relieve a headache. It can also be chewed to freshen breath, and to help you speak the truth. Keep fresh mint in your home to attract friendly spirits.

MINT RITUAL

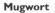

Place freshly chopped peppermint in the center of a white handkerchief, then tie all the corners together so that you have a parcel. Place it beneath your pillow for protection, healing, and prophetic dreams.

Marjoram

Ruled by the element air, marjoram has been used for centuries to promote love and peace. The ancient Greeks grew it in their gardens. If it flourished, that was the sign of a happy household that would attract many blessings; if it died, this did not bode well for the occupants of the house. Carrying marjoram is thought to prevent sickness and depression.

MARJORAM RITUAL

For a prosperous business and to promote good fortune, burn marjoram oil in your home and workplace. You can also add the essential oil to bathwater and soak whilst visualizing yourself being happy and successful.

Mugwort

Sacred to the Greek goddess Artemis (the Roman Diana), this powerful herb is part of the daisy family. It has antibacterial properties and is often used to treat wounds and skin allergies, and as an insect repellent. Some witches use mugwort stems as wands. Linked to the moon, mugwort will increase psychic powers and is also a great herb to carry for protection.

MUGWORT RITUAL

To prevent travel delays and keep you safe, keep a sprig of mugwort in the glovebox of your car, or in your pocket if you're traveling on foot. Hang fresh mugwort over your front and back doors to prevent intruders.

Oregano

Linked to the element air, oregano is popularly used in cooking and can help to promote peace and harmony. In some parts of the Mediterranean, magical practitioners would make a tea with oregano and use it to wash down the walls of their homes, as they believed it repelled evil. The ancient Greeks would crown newlyweds with it, to ensure a long and happy marriage.

☆ OREGANO RITUAL

Add a sprinkling of dried oregano to your regular floor wash. As you clean, visualize a stream of golden light sweeping into your home, bringing with it love and happiness.

Parsley

A good medicinal herb and easy to grow, parsley is most often used in protection spells. The Romans garnished their food with it because they believed it would protect them and prevent poisoning. It's also believed to promote lust and spice up a flagging sex drive. Introduce it into your diet by adding it to salads, stews, and soups.

☆ PARSLEY RITUAL

Either tie sprigs of parsley into a cheesecloth bag and add to running bathwater, or make up a brew by adding hot water to a handful of freshly chopped leaves in a cup and steeping them for five minutes. Strain the liquid into a jug and add to your bathtub. This powerful elixir will boost health and help you to feel strong and confident.

Sage

Ruled by the element air and linked to the god Jupiter (the Greek Zeus), sage is a great herb for healing and for cleansing the aura. Native Americans traditionally use sage in smudge sticks, which they burn to cleanse themselves. It makes an excellent natural toothpaste, and our ancestors would have rubbed sage leaves on their teeth to freshen their breath.

☆ SAGE RITUAL

Place a handful of fresh sage leaves in a bowl of hot water with a couple drops of bergamot essential oil. Carrying the bowl, move around your home, room by room, wafting the vapors into all corners and saying "I cleanse and protect this sacred space. My home is a happy, harmonious place!"

Rosemary

This powerful herb, ruled by the sun, is sacred to the Greek goddess of love, Aphrodite (the Roman Venus). Because of this, it's often used in love spells. The ancient Greeks also recognized its healing power, and it was used in rituals for protection and strength, and to maintain focus. It's believed that if you're struggling to concentrate, sniffing a sprig of fresh rosemary will give you clarity and focus.

ROSEMARY RITUAL

Before an exam or other important event, make a magical brew by adding sprigs of fresh rosemary to hot water with a few drops of lemon juice and a spoonful of honey. Stir, then leave to steep for a few minutes. Strain the liquid and sip it whilst picturing a clear head.

Thyme

This herb has a long tradition of being used in sacred rites, and is popular in midsummer rituals. It promotes psychic development and helps us to connect to the spiritual plane. Thyme is also used in love spells and is popular with fairy spirits. Ruled by Venus and linked to the element water, it makes a great magical tea.

THYME RITUAL

Place a piece of amethyst into a cup with a sprig of thyme. Add hot water and leave overnight on a window ledge in the light of the moon. In the morning, remove the stone and soak a flannel in the liquid. Place over your forehead for insightful visions of the future.

Vervain

Governed by Venus (the Greek Aphrodite), the scent of this herb is thought to be a powerful aphrodisiac. Associated with the summer solstice, it is sacred to druids, and is used in protection spells and to cleanse an area or magical tools before a ritual. It can help to overcome anxiety and negative emotions. It's also linked to poets, and can help you to tap into your creative side.

VERVAIN RITUAL

Steep a couple fresh vervain leaves in boiling water. Pour the liquid into a bowl and use to cleanse any crystals or stones that you use in magical work. Leave them in the vervain water overnight, along with any other tools, such as your athame or wand.

WORKING WITH PLANTS AND TREES

Throughout history, plants and flowers have been used in medicines and rituals to heal the sick and bring about positive change. Every living thing has a specific energy that can be used with a little magical know-how and skill. Below are some of the key plants and trees and their magical uses.

Aloe vera

This medicinal plant has many uses. The cooling gel from the leaves can be used to treat skin conditions and burns, reduce scarring, and moisturize the skin. Often hung over doors to attract good fortune into the home, this protective plant prevents harm and guards those who plant it from misfortune. It can also be placed under the pillow to aid sleep.

☆ ALOE VERA RITUAL

Place some fresh aloe on a window ledge with a lodestone (a natural magnetic stone), a whole nutmeg, and an acorn, to attract luck and happiness into your home. If you can't find a lodestone, a fridge magnet will do the same job.

Carnation

The Latin name for carnation, Dianthus, means "flower of Zeus," and this beautiful bloom lives up to its divine title. Often used to flavor ale and wine, the carnation has a spicy taste and is sometimes used to replace Indian spices. Magically, it's ruled by Jupiter and its element is fire, meaning that it is linked to action, success, luck, and fertility. The color of the carnation relates to its use in spells; for example, red carnations are linked to action and motivation, pink to compassion, orange to vitality and new energy, and white to protection and cleansing.

☆ CARNATION RITUAL

Keep a vase of fresh carnations on your altar. Choose colors that reflect your needs or spells that you're working on.

Catnip

Ruled by the Egyptian cat goddess Bast, and associated with the planet Venus, catnip is not just a treat for your feline friends. It's a great addition to any love spell and it also enhances natural beauty. It belongs to the mint family, and, when made into a medicinal tea, can help with digestion and menstrual cramps. Mixed with jasmine and lavender flowers and infused to make a magical bath, catnip will lift the spirits and soothe the soul.

☆ CATNIP RITUAL

Crush catnip leaves in the palm of your hand whilst thinking about the one you adore. Remove the leaves but do not rinse your hand; instead, hold your partner's hand and make a wish for your love to grow deeper.

Daffodil

The Romans believed that a special concoction made from daffodil roots could cure them of any ill, because it cleansed the system completely. These lovely yellow flowers are linked to rebirth and the element water. If you want to lift your spirits, spend some time gazing at daffodils in bloom. They are linked to purification and protection, so wear a daffodil about your person to attract good luck.

DAFFODIL RITUAL

Either keep a vase of fresh daffodils on your window ledge to attract friendly spirits and fairies into your home, or place pictures of daffodils in your living room and hallway.

Dandelion

Also known as cankerwort and blowball, dandelions have lots of practical uses. The root can be dried and roasted to make coffee or tea, which is caffeine-free and will promote psychic development. A tincture of dandelion makes a wonderful skin cleanser, and dandelion tea is thought to improve the digestion. It's also said that if you blow the seeds off the head of a dandelion and make a wish, it will come true.

DANDELION RITUAL

Soak a dandelion root in hot water, strain, and add a couple drops of lavender essential oil. Massage the water gently into your temples and your third eye, the area in the center of your forehead. Close your eyes and let any psychic visions or messages come to you.

Foxglove

This pretty flower, which is sacred to druids, is extremely toxic and should never be eaten. It is associated with fairies and the otherworld, and it is said that wherever you find foxgloves growing in the wild, you'll find fairies. In medieval times, witches would often use a special ointment made from foxgloves to help them experience flying dreams and hallucinations. If you have foxgloves in your garden, your house will be protected from intruders.

FOXGLOVE RITUAL

To inject some fairy magic into your life and bring about a pleasant surprise, find a patch of foxgloves growing in the wild. Leave a piece of quartz crystal in the middle of the flowers as an offering, whilst making a wish for fairy blessings.

Holly

Associated with the festive season, holly can be used at any time of year in spells for protection and to increase lust. It's thought that if a man carries a sprig of holly with him, he will become instantly irresistible. The berries are poisonous if eaten, but can be used in dyes for clothes. It's also believed that if you throw the berries at a wild animal, it will retreat or lie down.

HOLLY RITUAL

Soak a sprig of holly in cold water and leave out in the light of a full moon. The next day, splash the water all over your body to attract good fortune.

Garlic

Known for its protective and medicinal properties, garlic is a powerful addition to any herbal witch's garden. People traditionally wore garlic during times of plague, as they thought it could absorb disease. Roman soldiers often ate garlic before going into battle, believing that it would protect them and give them strength. It is sacred to the Greek goddess Hecate (the Roman Trivia), and eating a diet rich in garlic will bring good luck and keep evil at bay.

GARLIC RITUAL

Leave a fresh garlic bulb at a crossroads, and ask the goddess Hecate to remove any obstacles to success in your life.

Honeysuckle

If this flowering vine grows over your home, you'll always be protected and in good health. Honeysuckle is mostly toxic, but the sweet-smelling flowers can be used in spells and rituals for money, protection, and psychic power. The dried, powdered bark is often burned as incense on special occasions, such as sabbats, and the flowers can be crushed and massaged into the forehead to encourage psychic visions.

HONEYSUCKLE RITUAL

Surround a green candle with honeysuckle flowers and make a wish for more money. Let the candle burn down and then scatter the flowers over your front doorstep.

Marigold

This lovely flower is best picked when the sun is at its hottest. Used to ease the heart and mind, marigolds are often included in rituals for lost loved ones. It's thought that if a young girl touches the petals of a marigold with her bare feet, she will be able to understand the language of the birds. Marigolds are also believed to hold the key to good sight, and that staring at a field of marigolds will improve your vision.

MARIGOLD RITUAL

If you're facing any kind of judgment or legal problem, gather and dry marigold petals and carry them with you in a charm bag.

Mistletoe

Ruled by the sun, mistletoe is most sacred when found growing in the boughs of an oak tree. The berries are poisonous but can be dried, and were often thrown into the fire or added to charm bags for protection. The wood can be used to fashion wands. In medieval times, it was believed that if you hung mistletoe above a baby's cradle, the child was protected from fairies and evil spirits.

MISTLETOE RITUAL

Always tie mistletoe bundles with red ribbon or string. This increases its power and will attract abundance into the home.

Rose

This beautiful flower has long been associated with love, and is linked to the Roman goddess Venus and her Greek counterpart, Aphrodite. Used in Wiccan handfasting ceremonies and often worn by couples and guests, the rose is a symbol of union, love, beauty, and self-esteem. It is also linked to healing. Rose oil can be burned to generate amorous feelings, and a fresh red or pink rose can be placed on the altar when making love requests.

ROSE RITUAL

Invest in some rose water and spray it on clothes and hair before going on a date. This gorgeous scent promotes love and beauty, and also attracts admirers.

Sunflower

A symbol of the sun, this joyous flower brings happiness, success, and great wisdom. It can be used to treat depression, as it repels negative energy. Sunflower seeds increase fertility, so if you want to conceive, include them in your diet and sprinkle them on your altar. Growing sunflowers in your garden brings good luck and a happy harvest.

SUNFLOWER RITUAL

To make a wish come true, stand beneath the rising sun holding a sunflower in your hands. State your wish and then place the sunflower in a vase of water.

Violet

This pretty little flower is linked to love, serenity, and happiness. It's thought that if you pick the first violet of the spring, all your dreams will come true. Smelling and carrying violets can help to calm anger and bring contentment. Violets can be used with other herbs and flowers in rituals to attract true love.

VIOLET RITUAL

If you're seeking inspiration, keep a posy of fresh violets and lavender on your desk. This combination of flowers will raise the spirits and stimulate the mind.

TREES

The druids embraced the sacred power of
trees in their magical workings. They
conducted many of their ceremonies and
rituals in oak-lined glades. They knew that
each tree had a different type of energy
and a spirit, called a dryad, that inhabited it.
Trees are part of our natural landscape, and
remind us of the ancient forests that once
covered the land. They're timeless and
resolute, able to withstand change, yet
repeating their own cycle of transformation
each year. If you want to work with nature
and increase your knowledge of herbal
magic, it's important to acquaint yourself
with the power of trees, to experience and
work with their energy. A great deal of
information is available, but the best way
to learn is to spend time beneath the
branches of each tree. This brief guide
will help you to understand some of the
influences associated with different types
of tree, and their folklore.

Apple

The apple tree was
sacred to the Celts, who
believed that it represented love in all its forms. They would
decorate their bedchambers with apple blossom to
encourage love and romance. Because apples could be stored
for a long time and remain fresh, they were associated with
the deep power of true love, and the Greek goddess of love
and beauty, Aphrodite. It was also thought that apples could
be used to remove warts by cutting the ripe fruit into three
sections and rubbing it on the affected area.

APPLE RITUAL

*Take an apple and sit beneath an apple tree. As you eat,
think about love and what it means to you. If you're
searching for new love, imagine that you already have it. If
you just want to improve the flow of love in your life,
visualize yourself bathed in pink light. When you have eaten
the apple, thank the tree for giving you this gift.*

Ash

The druids believed that the sky and earth were connected by the ash tree. They were in
awe of its great height and its root system, and they understood that its energy was about
growth, and reaching higher realms. A protector of children, the ash was considered the
cradle of all life and linked to rebirth and renewal. If you wish to revamp an area of your life,
this is the tree to work with.

ASH RITUAL

*Find a strip of ash bark or a twig that has fallen from the tree and burn it in a fireproof dish.
The wood usually burns intensely, creating lots of energy. Watch the flames burn and imagine
them growing before your eyes. Imagine stepping into the fire, and feel the heat strip away any
negative emotions or thoughts. See yourself stepping out of the fire, renewed and rejuvenated.*

Beech

Historically, it was thought that if you carved a wish into a beech twig, it would come true. Ruled by the planet Mercury, beech is associated with communication and learning, and its twigs were often used as wands to connect with the spirit world. Medicinally, the leaves were sometimes used in poultices to treat skin conditions. If you need to learn something fast or want to increase your knowledge, work with the energy of this tree.

BEECH RITUAL

Collect fallen twigs from a beech tree and place them in a dish either on your altar or on your desk. Add a few drops of rosemary essential oil. Ask the beech tree to bless you with wisdom and clarity every day.

Birch

Druids would often carry the bark of the birch tree, which was associated with the sun, as kindling. They believed in its energy and strength, and recognized its adaptability—the fact that it seemed to be able to grow anywhere. For this reason it was often associated with passion, enthusiasm, and renewal. It's also used in spells for protection and to promote courage.

BIRCH RITUAL

Add a tiny piece of birch bark to a charm bag with a pinch each of salt and pepper. Say "Beautiful birch with your power clear, bless me with the strength to face my fear. Let confidence build within my soul, so that I may accomplish any goal." Keep the bag with you when you face challenges.

Hawthorn

Said to form a portal to the fairy realm, hawthorn is a magical tree linked to enchantment and wonder, and a guardian of springs and wells. The wood from this tree was once used to make maypoles. It is associated with love, purity, and fertility, and its blossoms are thought to incite lust, particularly in men. Because of its thorns, it is also used in protection spells. Work with the energy of this tree to increase desire, and to protect yourself from harmful influences.

HAWTHORN RITUAL

Take a thorn and a piece of blossom from this tree. Think about your current situation. Is anything holding you back? Are you helping yourself, or is there a part of your personality that you'd like to change for the better? Write down your thoughts and observations on some paper. Wrap the thorn and the blossom in the paper and place beneath the tree, asking the hawthorn for help and protection.

Hazel

A beautiful tree to work with, the hazel has many gifts, including poetry, divination, wisdom, and a sense of fun. The Celts believed that the air around a hazel tree is infused with magic and creativity. Because of this, hazel is often used to make wands; it is also very popular for divining rods. The leaves can be used in tinctures and brews to ease diarrhea and sickness. If you want to unleash your creativity and enchant the world with your talents, tap into this tree's vibrant energy.

☆ HAZEL RITUAL

Collect fallen hazelnuts, wash them, and grind them into a powder. Mix with a spoonful of honey and eat or sprinkle over vanilla ice cream and enjoy as a tasty treat. As you eat, give thanks to the hazel tree and ask for its blessings upon you.

Oak

The oak is a noble tree associated with strength, endurance, faith, and determination. It was sacred to the druids, who, inspired by the mighty roots that supported it, believed that it could promote courage against all the odds. It is said that King Arthur's round table was made from oak wood. Medicinally, the bark was used to treat wounds and skin conditions. If you wish to turn your fortune around, or you need a power boost, this is the tree to call on.

☆ TREE RITUAL

Stand beneath the boughs of an oak tree and take a minute to soak up the energy. When you're ready, sit with your back to the trunk of the tree. Feel its power passing into you and lighting you up from the inside. Give thanks for its strength. Finally, if you can, find an acorn or a piece of bark and carry it with you to attract good fortune.

Rowan

Linked to the sun because of its ability to grow on hilltops and craggy inclines, the rowan or mountain ash is the tree of magic and inspiration. The Celts believed that it represented the hidden mysteries of nature, and used it in sacred rites and rituals. Its twigs were often used as divining rods, and witches would fashion wands from its wood. The berries are packed with vitamin C and often used in tea to ease the symptoms of colds. Rowan can help you to see the magic all around and increase your personal power.

ROWAN RITUAL

Take a handful of rowan berries and any fallen twigs and carry them to a river or stream. Say "Sweet rowan with your vibrant berry, lift my soul and make me merry. Show the magic all around, as stream meets river, and sky meets ground." Throw the berries and twigs into the flowing water.

Willow

This mystical tree is governed by the moon and linked to feminine energy and divination. Medicinally, the bark is used to make aspirin, and infusions of the bark were used centuries ago to cure fever. Often called the tree of immortality because of its ability to grow from a fallen branch, the willow is associated with moon magic, love, and healing. Witches' brooms are often made from its wood. Work with the energy of this tree if you want to enhance your personal and psychic power.

WILLOW RITUAL

Willow branches and twigs are usually quite flexible. Bind a fallen branch or stick into a loose knot, saying "Empower me, sweet willow tree, and let me see what is to be." Repeat the chant three times whilst standing in the light of the moon.

Yew

One of the most ancient of all trees, the yew is the tree of immortality. It's a symbol of regeneration and is linked to rebirth and transformation. It is so often found in graveyards because it was thought that its roots would spread to the mouths of the dead, helping them to be reborn. Often used in protection spells and to contact the spirits of the dead, this powerful tree can help you to contact other realms and develop your spiritual nature.

YEW RITUAL

Sit beneath a yew tree with a photograph or memento of a lost loved one. Spend a few minutes thinking about the person and the memories you shared. Look up into the branches of the tree and speak out loud a message for your loved one. Remember to give thanks to the tree for passing it on to the spirit world.

CHAPTER 4

ELEMENTAL MAGIC

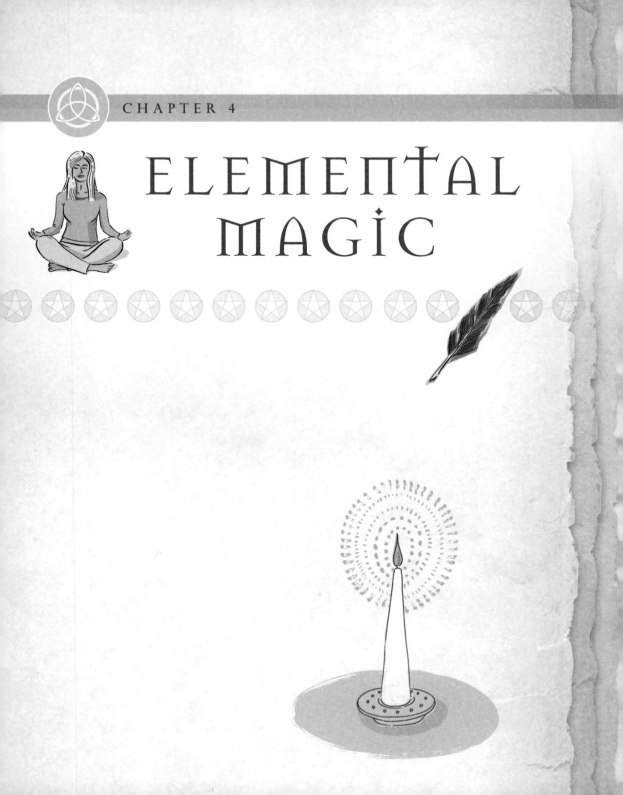

Connecting with the Elements

An important aspect of the Wiccan path is about developing a connection with the four elements: earth, air, fire, and water. These elements, which make up the entire universe, form the basis of all magic and represent the four quarters of the magical circle. Learning about these elements and how to work with them is key for anyone with an interest in witchcraft. You may find that you are naturally drawn to this type of magic, instinctively work with the elements every day, and understand the key principles of each area and what they represent. You may even find that you're particularly drawn to one of the elements, and find yourself working with this energy and using it as you go about your daily business. For example, people who have high-flying jobs that involve lots of action, swift decisions, and leadership taps into the fire element to reach their goals. This is perfectly natural.

The elements form the basis of our personality, and some of us have more of one than of the others. This is evident in the way we think, feel, and act.

Getting Started

Although the elements are part of our daily life, it can be difficult to know how to start to connect to them more deeply as part of your Wiccan practice. As you begin to work with the elements, you will realize that there are lots of simple steps that you can incorporate into your daily life to bring you closer to their universal power.

- Explore each individual element. Spend some time in its presence, and think about what it means to you and how it features in your life.

- Embrace the weather as this is an important part of elemental magic. Air features in the wind, water in rain, and fire in the sun, and the earth is affected by all three. So get outside in all types of weather and let your senses take over. Notice how you feel when it's sunny, raining, or blowing a gale.

- Play a game. If you could control an element, which one would it be and why? Simply by asking this question, you'll gain a deeper understanding of how each one works.

- Match colors to the elements and include all four in your home. For example, you might want the soothing water element in your bedroom, so you'd include silvery blue tones and aquamarine. Or you might choose to have an earthy feel to your living room, so you'd pick green and brown shades for your decor.

- Tap into your creative side and write down your thoughts and feelings during a storm or on a hot, sunny day. Use your imagination and create a poem or ode to each element, then use it to connect with the power of the element in a ritual.

On the following pages, I outline what each element represents and how to work with it. As always, nothing is set in stone. Trust your intuition and develop your own way of connecting with the elements. Invite them into your life and recognize their power, and you will find that it becomes second nature to use them in your magical work.

Earth

The earth is the mother of all things and the spirit of creation, central to every living thing. Strong and steady, this is the most nurturing element because it provides stability for and sustains all life, from plants and trees to animals and humans. Other elements can affect the earth—for example, excess water may make it wet and marshy, or lots of sunshine (the fire element) may cause drought—but the earth still exists and comes first. It is associated with new growth, prosperity, strength, and stamina, and so working with this element can improve the flow of abundance in your life, and help to keep you grounded. It is linked to feminine power and represents the womb, so if you want to improve your fertility or sow the seeds for a better future, connect to Mother Earth.

EARTH ASSOCIATIONS

COLOR	Brown, green
DIRECTION	North
PLACES	Meadows, fields, forests, gardens, farms, caves
STONES	Amber, coal
PLANTS	Almost anything that grows, including moss and grass
MAGICAL TOOL	Broomstick
DEITIES	Gaia, Persephone (Roman Proserpina)

ACTIVATE THE EARTH ELEMENT

Take a piece of amber or quartz crystal and some wild-flower seeds out into the yard. If you don't have a yard, you can perform this ritual using a large plant pot filled with earth or compost. Dig a hole with your hands in the earth, noticing how it feels against your skin as you do so. Notice how alive it makes you feel, and enjoy those warm sensations. Sprinkle the seeds into the hole and add the crystal. Say "Mighty Mother Earth, I feel your presence here. I welcome you into my life, I sense your power near. I'm supported by your strength and love in everything I do. With every day I walk this earth, I give my thanks to you." Cover the hole with more earth or compost and pat it down. Spend a few minutes with your hands palm down on the earth, and repeat the chant.

Other ways to connect to the earth element:

- Go for a walk every day, and think about the rhythm as your feet hit the ground and connect with the earth.

- Hug a tree or spend some time beneath its branches. Also sit with your back against the trunk.

- Collect interesting stones, twigs, and leaves, and put them in a decorative dish as a table display to remind you of your connection with the earth.

- Stand barefoot outside and imagine roots growing from the soles of your feet, anchoring you to the earth.

- Mow the lawn and tend to the garden by weeding and raking the earth.

- Get to know a bit about wildlife and do your bit to conserve it. For example, you might want to create a bug hotel out of old bits of wood, or put up a bird box.

Air

This is one of the easier elements to connect with: we take in air every day as we breathe. It's already an important part of our life—we need it to survive—and as we take in each breath, we're working with its immense power. Its presence can be felt in the breeze on our skin and seen in the rustling leaves of trees. It is the spirit that moves in all things and an active magical force that governs the intellect. Closely linked to manifestation and communication, air is light and active. Think of Hermes, the fleet-footed Greek god (Roman Mercury), who would fly through the air delivering messages. He is the epitome of this element. Sound, the way it travels on the breeze and lifts our spirits, is also closely linked to air. If you want to engage your imagination, communicate new ideas, and be inspired, air is the element to work with.

AIR ASSOCIATIONS

COLOR	Yellow
DIRECTION	East
PLACES	Mountains, clifftops, towers, anywhere else outdoors
STONES	Citrine, quartz
HERB	Dill
MAGICAL TOOL	Wand
DEITIES	Arianrhod, Hermes (Roman Mercury)

ACTIVATE THE AIR ELEMENT

Gather a handful of feathers and stand outside, if possible on top of a hill or mountain. Hold the feathers in both hands and offer them up to the air by raising your cupped hands toward the sky. Say "I embrace the element of air. I let it feed my soul. I feel it flow around me, nourishing my whole. I activate the element of air. I move with lightness and ease. Inspired and brimming with new ideas, like a gentle spring breeze." Now spin around whilst throwing the feathers into the air. When you've finished, spend a few minutes breathing deeply. You should feel both calm and energized.

Other ways to connect to the element of air:

• Fly a kite on a windy day. The wind will take charge of the direction. At the same time, ask it to help you go with the flow in your own life.

• Try hill-walking or climbing mountains. The closer you feel to the sky, the more in tune you will be with the element.

• Hang out your laundry. Notice how the wind rapidly dries your clothes, leaving them crisp and fresh, just as it can clear a path for you and refresh your soul.

• Try birdwatching. Notice how the birds navigate a path through the air, and adopt the same approach to each day.

• Learn to breathe properly, taking in a deep breath and slowly releasing it.

• Open all the windows in your house on a windy day and let the breeze blow through and cleanse the space.

Fire

This masculine element is all about movement and transformation. Fire creates smoke, ash, and heat. It can be destructive when it gets out of hand, but it is also extremely useful. It performs numerous functions, from providing warmth and light on a cold winter's night, to helping us cook our food. Fire is linked to passion, movement, and leadership. Its potent energy can help us to direct our magical intent and grow in confidence and give us the drive we need to achieve great things and make our dreams come true. It brings us together, as we sit around the fire and share our tales. Working with this element brings fast results and helps us to tap into the very spark of life, from which we all came.

FIRE ASSOCIATIONS

COLORS	Orange, red
DIRECTION	South
PLACES	Volcanoes, open fires and ovens, candles, the bedroom
STONES	Carnelian, jasper
PLANTS	Cacti, chili plants
MAGICAL TOOL	Athame
DEITIES	Aine, Hestia, Pele,

ACTIVATE THE FIRE ELEMENT

Using your athame or a pin, carve your name or initials into the wax of a red candle. Massage a drop of sunflower oil into the candle whilst thinking about the element fire and what it means to you. Think of all the words that you associate with fire, and how they relate to you and your approach to life. Perhaps you need more fiery energy to help you to move forward or fulfill a dream; or maybe you already work with this element and need to control its energy in your world. Light the candle and say "As the flame grows, my spirit soars. I feel the warmth as the fire roars. I welcome your power into my life; may your energy rid me of any strife." As the candle burns down, imagine that you're surrounded by a protective circle of fire.

Other ways to connect to the element of fire:

• Sit in front of an open fire and gaze at the flames. Feel the heat filling you with energy to fulfill your magical desires.

• Light a candle and imagine that you're relighting the spark of life inside you.

• Burn some herbs and waft the smoke around your body to cleanse your aura.

• Put on a hot tune and dance as though no one is watching. This promotes action and helps you to get in touch with your primitive, passionate side.

• Immerse yourself in red and orange by redecorating rooms in these colors or just update your wardrobe to inspire some magical action.

• Hold a storytelling event in your backyard and light a fire that you can sit around and share your tales.

Water

Water supports us, and we need it to survive. Our bodies are 50–65 percent water, meaning that it has a huge influence on how we think and feel. Water is related to the emotions, so it affects the way we interact with others, and it can cleanse and refresh the spirit. Those who feel a great deal of empathy tend to be "water people." They instinctively know and can identify with another person's feelings, and find it easy to walk in their shoes. Water is the most sensitive element; it flows into and out of our lives, just as people and things come and go. Water is transient, and transformative. It can bring things to us, and it can help us to release the things we no longer need. It's therefore the best element to work with for manifestation. A feminine element, water is most often associated with love, healing, intuition, and cleansing.

WATER ASSOCIATIONS

COLORS	Aquamarine, blue, silver
DIRECTION	West
PLACES	Oceans, rivers, streams, wells, ponds, lakes, waterfalls, fountains, showers, baths, steam rooms, saunas
STONES	Aquamarine, clear quartz
PLANT	Water lily
MAGICAL TOOLS	Cauldron, chalice
DEITIES	Aphrodite (Roman Venus), Oshun, Yemaya

ACTIVATE THE WATER ELEMENT

Take a chalice, goblet, or magical cup that you use specifically for rituals to a stream or pond. Spend a few minutes looking at the water. Note how freely it flows and how it nourishes and replenishes the land. Invite the element into your life by giving thanks for its presence. Say "Water, you flow freely into my life, giving me strength, power, and inspiration. Your love is never-ending, as you cleanse my soul. I open my heart to you now and give thanks for your presence in my life." Fill the cup with water from the stream. Dip both hands into the water and let it trickle through your fingers. Repeat the magical chant and then cast the remaining water back into the stream.

Other ways to connect to the element of water:

• Visit the sea or a lake or river whenever you can, and let the atmosphere wash over you.

• Walk in the rain and embrace the feeling of the raindrops on your face.

• When you bathe, immerse yourself in the water, close your eyes and imagine that you're cocooned in loving energy.

• Collect fresh rainwater (the first rainfall of spring is supposed to be especially powerful) and use it in a hair rinse, or splash on your face for instant invigoration.

• Go swimming regularly and feel the strength of the water supporting your body.

• Drink plenty of water throughout the day, so that you're alert, hydrated, and full of magical energy.

• Imagine that you're standing beneath a waterfall of energy. Feel the water hit the top of your head and shower your body in white healing light.

The Fifth Element: Spirit

Also known as "Akasha," or "inner space," the fifth element binds everything together. It is the force of all life. It also represents the collective unconscious, and knowledge of the past, present, and future. Thinking of the universe as a giant library, which contains records of every thought and deed, will give you an idea of what the collective unconscious represents. Akasha's divine essence is the spark of life, the soul that sits in our physical body. Its energy is all about creation and change, and it represents the unknown. It is such a vast and far-reaching element that it has no general direction, and it's difficult to associate it with stones or herbs, but the colors purple, indigo, or black are often used when talking about spirit.

ACTIVATE THE SPIRIT ELEMENT

Imagine you're sitting in a circle that corresponds to the four elements (earth, air, fire, and water). If it helps, you can mark it out with stones or crystals. Visualize a stream of purple light coming down from the sky and hitting the top of your head. This represents the fifth element, spirit. Feel this energy surround you in a funnel of light, and flow through you. Spend a few minutes noticing how you feel. Give thanks for this element by saying "May the spirit within shine bright and radiate love. May the universe support me and bring blessings from above." Record any thoughts, feelings, or images that come to you, as they may be messages from the spirit world.

Other ways to connect to the spirit element:

- Simply being alive connects you to this element, so embrace every minute of every day.

- Introduce some regular quiet time into your daily schedule. Switch off phones and computers, close the door, and focus on your breath. Let thoughts come and go, and use the time to access and nurture your inner space.

- Become more aware of spirit. Reach out to lost loved ones by lighting a candle and talking to them. Imagine them standing before you in spirit form.

- Attempt astral projection by imagining that you're looking down on your sleeping body. See yourself standing at the end of your bed, a spirit entity attached to your physical form.

- Notice your dreams and work with them. Before you go to sleep, ask the spirit world to send you a sign or message in a dream.

CHAPTER 5

MOON
MAGIC

The Power of the Moon

Shining bright in the sky, the moon has fascinated humankind for centuries. It features in folklore and mythology from around the world, and is an important influence in magical workings. Astrologically, it's linked to the emotions and the element water, and it also rules the tides. Since the beginning of time, humans have made up stories to explain its existence and the way it changes shape. They have tried to work with its power, have been charmed by its effects—claiming temporary madness during a full moon—and have even tried to catch it. Every mythology has deities—usually female—that are linked to the moon, and more often than not they govern magic and wisdom. The moon helps us to get in touch with our feminine side and develop intuition. It helps us to engage our imagination and introduce a little creativity into our world. This mystical object is part of our life, and we can work with its energy to enhance spells and manifest the things we need.

If you're a natural Moon Witch, you'll already feel attuned to the moon's power and feel its effects more keenly than others. Perhaps you have vivid dreams during the night of a full moon, or you can feel your energy level fade as the moon wanes. You could be drawn to magical rituals that take place in the light of the moon, or you might simply be fascinated by some of the folklore attached to this glistening orb. Whatever your interest, it's definitely worth exploring the phases of the moon and learning how to work with them to get the most out of your magic. Explore some of the ideas in this chapter, and if it feels right to you, go with the flow and let the light of the moon lead the way.

Working with the Moon: Getting Started

The best way to get to know the moon's power and work with it is to experience it first hand. This means getting out into the light of the moon and spending time in its presence.

- Simply sitting by a window and gazing up at the moon is a good start. Use this time to relax and quiet your mind. Listen to the rhythm of your breathing and let thoughts or images come to you. Ask the moon to bless you with inspiration and, if you feel the urge, put pen to paper and write down whatever comes to mind.

- Get to know the folklore surrounding the moon. Pick out your favorite tales and ask yourself why you like them. Do they strike a chord with you? Perhaps you feel connected to that specific mythology, or maybe you have an affinity with the ideas and feelings associated with the moon. Have fun exploring history and learning about this amazing entity.

- Invest in a piece of moonstone. Charge it by leaving it out all night in the light of a full moon. Wear it whenever possible to feel connected to the moon.

The Phases of the Moon

If we chart the progress of the moon, we notice the way it changes. Growing from nothing into a full moon is called waxing; and slowly changing back into a crescent moon and fading is called waning. When the moon appears to vanish completely from the sky, this is called the "dark of the moon." It then begins the monthly cycle again. Each phase of the moon is important and can be used magically to enhance the working of a spell.

New moon • Waxing crescent • Waxing half first quarter • Waxing gibbous • Full moon • Waning gibbous • Waning half last quarter • Waning crescent

The Dark of the Moon

Ruled by the crone aspect of the triple goddess, the dark of the moon is a time for reflection. It's the deepest, darkest point, when the moon seems to disappear from the sky. It's a time to look into your soul, to be honest, and embrace the darker elements of your psyche. Use the power of the dark of the moon to help you to let go of things and people that are no longer any good for you. Be honest with yourself and others. Let this period help you to uncover hidden truths, so that you're ready to embrace a new beginning.

Dark of the Moon Ritual

Hold a piece of obsidian in your hands. This black stone is known for its protective powers. Breathe in deeply and, as you breathe out, imagine that you're pouring any negative thoughts into the stone. If you're trying to release something from your life, imagine that the stone is absorbing it. Take the stone outside and offer it to the moon. Say "I offer this to you this night, to symbolize my plight. That which is no good has gone away, as the dark of the moon has swallowed the day." Bury the obsidian deep in the earth and say "Drawn into the belly of the earth, to begin the journey of rebirth. By the power of the dark of the moon I am released, not a moment too soon. So mote it be!"

NEW MOON

You can hardly see it at this stage, but the moon has been reborn. Like the first days of spring, the new moon has arrived and is about to grow and blossom in the sky. There's a hint of optimism, a feeling of renewed hope in the air. This is the perfect time to work magic for new beginnings. If you're looking for change, now is the time to grasp it. Be bold and work spells that will help you to move on to a new and exciting chapter in your life.

NEW MOON RITUAL

Take a piece of paper and imagine that you're writing an outline of a chapter in the book of your life. This is a new chapter, so write down all the things you'd like to do in it. You can make it as exciting as you like. Take the paper outside and look up at the sky. Imagine that you're talking to the moon, and read the list out loud. When you've finished, say "As the new moon's light rains down on me, these things I speak, so they shall be!"

WAXING MOON

When the moon starts to get bigger, it's in its waxing phase. It's building steadily to a full moon, and with every day it gets brighter and more powerful. The optimism that was hinted at during the new moon is now in full flow.

Energy is building and there's a feeling of striding out into the unknown to make a difference. This period of growth is a great time to work spells that attract or increase something in your life. If you're looking for new love or just want to increase your bank balance, this is the time to work your magic.

WAXING MOON RITUAL

Use the power of the waxing moon to increase the flow of love, money, luck, or happiness into your life. Plant wild-flower seeds in the ground by the light of the moon, placing a piece of moonstone or quartz crystal in the earth with them. As you do so, picture what you want and see yourself with it. Imagine how you'd feel and then give thanks to the moon for helping you to attract your heart's desire. Pat the earth down and water the area, then say "Mother moon, let your light shine. Bless me with your gifts divine. What I see, may it come true, through the power that flows from you. So mote it be!"

Wiccan Wisdom

If you're a keen baker, have a go at making bread during the waxing moon. As the dough rises in the oven, visualize the moon getting bigger and showering you in positive energy.

FULL MOON

The moon has reached its pinnacle: it is at its fullest and brightest in the sky. The perfect circle of light illuminates the darkness as it reaches the peak of its power. There's a definite buzz about a full moon. The energy is vibrant and alive and, if you're particularly attuned to it, you'll also feel a heightened sense of adventure and the promise of exciting things to come. This giddiness is often referred to as "moon madness," and you may feel more creative on these nights. This is the time to reach for the stars. Go for your dreams and work magical wish spells.

FULL MOON RITUAL

Stand in the light of the full moon. As you gaze at it shining in the sky, imagine a shower of white light pouring over you. Stretch your arms up and open them as if you're embracing the power of the moon. Breathe deeply and imagine drinking in that power; feel it flooding your entire body with light. Say "Upon this night with the full moon bright, my hopes and dreams are in my sight. Guide me well, as I say this spell. May your blessings fall, as I heed your call."

Wiccan Wisdom

On the night of the full moon, create a circular space using stones, crystals, or a mat to mark the area. Spend some time sitting here in quiet contemplation with your eyes closed, meditating on the image of the moon.

WANING MOON

As the moon begins to decrease in size, you may feel a dip in energy. It's heading towards the dark of the moon, and a period of rest. Everything is slowing down, the frantic energy of the full moon has come to a head, and there's a feeling of restraint. The universe breathes a sigh of relief and begins to wind down. Use this time to release things in your life that you no longer need. Work with the moon's energy to help you to cut ties and break bad habits.

WANING MOON RITUAL

This ritual will help you to break a bad habit. Take a small stone or piece of paper to represent the habit you'd like to break. Place it in a bowl of water, take the bowl outside, and place it on the ground in the light of the moon. Walk around the bowl three times whilst saying "By the power of the waning moon, this habit be gone, not a moment too soon. So mote it be!" Throw the water on the ground where it can be soaked up, and toss the stone or paper away.

DRAWING DOWN THE MOON

This ritual, often performed when a full moon s in the sky, or during the dark of the moon, is about drawing the power of the goddess into the practitioner. Many covens perform this ritual, with the high priest drawing down the moon so that the high priestess can be infused with the power of the goddess. Incantations are usually made to the three aspects of the triple goddess: the maiden, the mother, and the crone. Once she is invoked, the practitioner may feel a surge of energy, and sometimes the goddess will speak through her.

DRAWING DOWN THE MOON RITUAL

Some followers of the Wiccan path believe that this is best done in a coven, but a solitary practitioner may choose to perform this ritual to feel empowered and connected to the goddess.

The best way to do this is from the heart. Start by thinking about what the word "goddess" means to you and how the moon's feminine power gives you strength. Imagine that you're writing an ode to the moon. Give thanks for her energy and celebrate the goddess at the same time. You might begin by saying "Great mother moon, goddess of the night sky, I give thanks for your light and energy. I ask that you join me. Fill my heart and mind with your divine power." If you have an altar, you can perform this ritual standing in front of it, with your arms crossed over your chest. Alternatively, stand outside and gaze up at the moon whilst making your incantation. When you feel ready, open your arms as if embracing the power of the goddess.

Moon Deities

Every culture has its own moon myths, and most have a deity associated with the moon. Here are some of the most popular, along with suggestions of how to work with them.

HECATE

This Greek moon goddess is often called the queen of the witches. She's associated with magic, witchcraft, divination, and ancient wisdom. A powerful triple goddess, meaning she embraces the three aspects—maiden, mother, and crone— Hecate usually appears in her "crone" form. The best time to appeal to her for help with your spells is during the dark of the moon, when she's particularly helpful at removing obstacles.

TRY THIS

Visit a crossroads late at night and leave an offering to Hecate, such as a flower, a crystal, or a poem you've written. Ask her for an insight into or vision of the future.

ISIS

This beautiful Egyptian moon deity is associated with magic, wisdom, medicine, and beauty. Known for her intelligence and charm, Isis managed to trick the sun god Ra into revealing his secret name so that she could steal his power. A warm and giving goddess, she makes a point of teaching her people new skills and passing on her knowledge.

TRY THIS

Isis is associated with the sycamore or maple tree, and her stone is lapis lazuli. Place a piece of lapis beneath the branches of a sycamore tree on the night of a full moon and make a wish for Isis to bless you with ancient wisdom and assist you in your magical work.

RHIANNON

Rhiannon is the bewitching Welsh goddess of the moon. Often called the divine queen of the fairies, Rhiannon would appear on a beautiful white horse dressed in silver robes. She married a mortal prince and they had a child, but he was cruelly kidnapped, leaving Rhiannon to take the blame for his murder. She bore the punishment (to carry visitors on her back to the castle) with humility, despite being innocent.

TRY THIS

Add a couple drops of geranium essential oil—associated with Rhiannon—to a tablespoon (15 ml) of sweet almond oil. Massage it into the wax of a white candle and then light the wick. Ask Rhiannon to bless you with an open heart and mind so that you can intuitively connect to others.

MOON ASSOCIATIONS

The associations listed below are strongly linked to the moon. Using them, or channeling their power, in your lunar spells will deepen your connection to the moon.

STONES	Moonstone, quartz
SCENTS	Frankincense, jasmine
ASTROLOGICAL SIGN	Cancer
COLORS	Silver, white

OTHER CELESTIAL OBJECTS

It's not just the moon that can affect your magic; the planets and other objects in the solar system have an influence, too. If you're drawn to astrological magic, do some research and find out which planets and other bodies you can work with, and how. Here are the most prominent ones and their associations.

MARS

The fiery red planet is associated with war, action, and the element fire, governed by the Roman god Mars (Greek Ares), and linked to the month of March. If you want swift action, this is the planet to work with. Its energy will help you to assert yourself and beat the competition.

STONES	Bloodstone, carnelian, garnet
SCENTS	Ginger, juniper
ASTROLOGICAL SIGN	Aries
COLOR	Red

MARS RITUAL

Tie red cotton or ribbon three times around a piece of ginger root. Say "Mars, warrior planet, may your fiery energy bless my soul. Give me strength and confidence to achieve my goal." Keep the ginger with you as a charm to connect you to the planet's energy.

VENUS

Venus is the planet of love and beauty, and associated with the Roman goddess of the same name, and her Greek counterpart, Aphrodite. Friday is linked to this planet, and is the best day to perform spells that tap into its energy. Whether you're looking for new love, to strengthen existing bonds, or simply to love yourself a bit more, this is the planet to work with.

STONES	Emerald, rose quartz
SCENTS	Geranium, rose
ASTROLOGICAL SIGNS	Taurus, Libra
COLORS	Blue, green, pink

☆ VENUS RITUAL

Place a pink rose in a vase with some water and sprinkle a circle of sugar around the vase. Make a wish for love. Take a piece of rose quartz and place it over your heart whilst giving thanks for all the love already in your life.

THE SUN

Vibrant and full of energy, the sun is associated with numerous deities, including the Egyptian sun god Ra and the Norse sun goddess Sunna. It is a powerful influence for success, power, happiness, and all-round vitality. Sunday is the best day to perform spells and rituals to connect with its energy, although its influence can be felt every day when the sun is out.

STONES	Amber, citrine
SCENTS	Orange, sandalwood
ASTROLOGICAL SIGN	Leo
COLORS	Gold, orange, yellow

☆ SUN RITUAL

Welcome the sun into your life every morning by throwing back the curtains, stretching your arms wide, and imagining a ray of golden light traveling from the sun directly into your chest area. Say "Glorious sun shining so bright, I welcome your joy and embrace your light."

MERCURY

Mercury is the planet of communication and commerce. Its influence is most prominent on Wednesdays, and it is associated with the Greek messenger god Hermes, equivalent to Mercury in Roman mythology. Work with this planet's energy when you want to perform spells to improve communication in relationships and business and if you wish to boost your personal charm and creativity.

STONE	Agate
SCENTS	Lavender, rosemary
ASTROLOGICAL SIGNS	Gemini, Virgo
COLOR	Orange

MERCURY RITUAL

Place a piece of agate in a cup with hot water and a sprig of fresh rosemary. Let the liquid steep for five minutes, then remove the stone and the rosemary and sip while asking Mercury to bless you with charm and creativity.

JUPITER

Associated with the element of fire, Jupiter is the largest planet in the solar system. Because of this, it's linked to the Roman king of the gods, Jupiter, and his Greek counterpart, Zeus. This immensely powerful planet can help you to increase your finances, generate success, and rejuvenate your life, but only if you have the best intentions. It's best to work with Jupiter on a Thursday, as this is the day most associated with it.

STONES	Amethyst, lapis lazuli
SCENTS	Cinnamon, frankincense
ASTROLOGICAL SIGN	Sagittarius
COLORS	Blue, purple

JUPITER RITUAL

Mix a couple drops of frankincense essential oil into a tablespoon (15 ml) of sunflower oil and massage into the wax of a blue candle. Light the candle, and place a gold coin next to it. Say "I call on Jupiter to turn things around. May wealth and abundance now abound."

CHAPTER 6

KITCHEN MAGIC

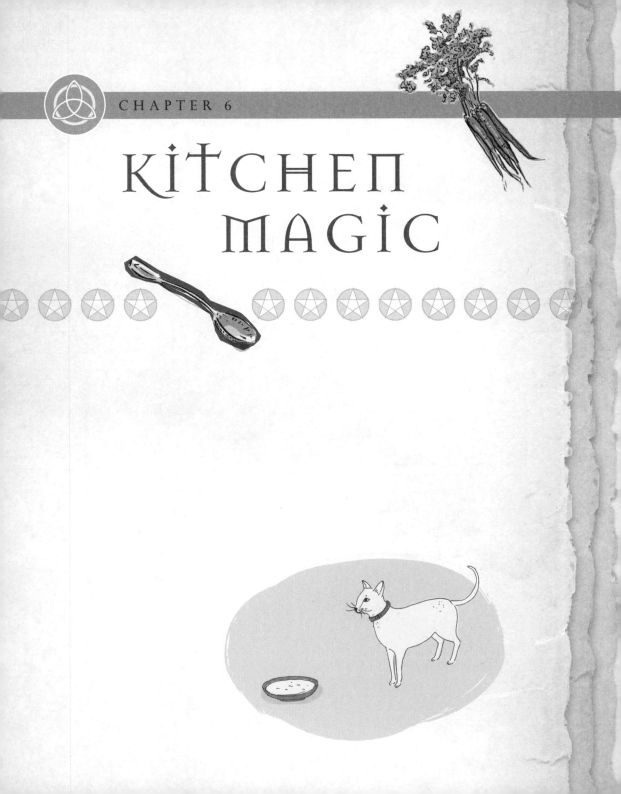

The Importance of the Kitchen

The kitchen is the heart of any home. It's the place where everyone comes together, and where they receive sustenance and nourishment. It's the fiery hearth, and the space where you cook meals for yourself and your family. So already it's a place of magic and creation. It's no surprise, then, that kitchen witchery has become popular in the Wiccan tradition. This is not a new concept. Wise women of old would spend time preparing warming meals on the stove, whilst infusing them with magical intentions. After all, a spell is like a recipe. It's a combination of ingredients mixed to manifest a certain outcome. We cook meals in the hope that they make us feel good, and ultimately keep us fit and well, so that is our desired outcome even if we don't purposely think of it at the time.

Some practitioners are drawn to this area because they're natural cooks, and enjoy the challenge of baking and creating, or experimenting with ingredients. Others might feel more at home working with the elements or the planets, but it's still important to explore kitchen witchery, if only to infuse your meals with extra love.

Getting Started with Kitchen Magic

To enhance the role of the kitchen and make it a magical place, think first about the function of the room. It's used for cooking, and it may also be used for eating and socializing. Maximize space and remove all clutter so that you can work effectively in the area and so that positive energy can flow.

- The kitchen is the heart of the home, so it's important to reflect this and look after it. Keep it clean and ordered—no piles of unwashed dishes in the sink!

- You might like to keep tools and implements that you'll be using for magical work separate from your normal household items.

- Create a special altar that can be adapted to suit your needs. This could be a small table or shelf, which you adorn with candles, herbs, crystals, and maybe a statue of the goddess. You can also use this space to keep your magical utensils.

- In days of old, the hearth was the place where food was cooked and spells worked. Today, the oven and hob provide a similar function. Try to look at them with fresh eyes and see the potential for the things you can manifest.

- Consider the color and decor of your kitchen. In general, light, airy colors are good for all kinds of magic. Blue is great for healing, green for money, and pink or red for love. You might choose to have different-colored cooking pots for working different types of magic.

Everyday Ingredients

As a Kitchen Witch, you'll start to understand that every ingredient contains energy that can be used in spells and rituals. You'll discover the folklore associated with certain foods, and from this you'll instinctively know how to use those foods to manifest positive change. To get you started, here's a guide to some of the most common foods and ingredients, and how they can be used.

CUPBOARD BASICS

These staples have surprising magical properties. Experiment and have fun with your cooking, while improving your Kitchen Witch skills.

Milk

Ruled by the moon and the element water, and associated with the emotions, milk is often used as an offering to the mother goddess in magical rites and rituals. The cow was sacred to the ancient Egyptians, who associated it with their goddess of wisdom and magic, Isis. Because of this, milk was often used in sacred rituals. Drinking milk can strengthen any relationship and smooth troubled waters.

☆ TRY THIS

On the night of a full moon, add a couple ice cubes to a glass of milk. Sip slowly whilst giving thanks to the moon deities for blessing you with intuition and creativity.

Bread

Wheat has been used for centuries in magical rites. Associated with the earth and often used in rituals to earth deities, bread—particularly wheatgerm bread—is thought to promote prosperity, fertility, and new growth. Baking bread is particularly powerful if you visualize your aim during all the stages of preparation, then watch as it browns in the oven. Different types of bread can be used for different things; garlic bread, for instance, is great for health and protection spells, and rye bread can be used in love spells.

☆ TRY THIS

Crumble a slice of bread into a dish. Take the crumbs outside and scatter them in a circle around you whilst saying "Great joy is mine, abundance divine. I'm blessed with wealth, prosperity, and health!"

Eggs

Eggs appear in folklore around the world. They're a symbol of creation, and are considered sacred because of this. They represent the ongoing cycle of life. The ancient Egyptians would swap decorated eggs at the time of the spring equinox as a way of embracing the spirit of renewal. In many pagan traditions, eggs are used for protection and healing, and practitioners would visualize a psychic egg as a shield to repel negative influences.

TRY THIS

Take an egg and roll it over your body, from the top of your head down to your feet. Imagine that the egg is soaking up any negative emotions. When you're finished, crack the egg into some newspaper. Say "I let you go, I shed this shell. I break the egg, so all is well."

Cheese

Cheese has been around for thousands of years— pieces have even been discovered in Egyptian tombs. Ruled by Saturn and linked to the element earth, cheese has many magical uses. Because of its consistency, hard cheese can be carved with symbols and used in rituals and spells. White cheese is associated with the moon and often shaped into a crescent moon. Soft cheese can be smeared in a specific pattern on bread and eaten whilst you visualize your desire.

TRY THIS

Take a piece of cheese and carve a heart into it. Cut the piece in half and serve to your heart's desire on a slice of tomato, also associated with love. As you eat the other half, picture the pair of you together.

Sugar

Sugar is linked to the planet Venus, and is used in spells to attract and sweeten, making it especially successful in love spells. It's thought that the god of agriculture, Kane, first brought sugar to Hawaii where it was used in rituals for love and success. Linked to the element water and to the emotions, sugar can be used in moderation to sweeten relationships and give them a boost. In folklore, knocking over a sugar bowl is a sign that money is coming your way, and accidentally mixing up sugar and salt in a recipe means that good news will arrive soon.

TRY THIS

Light a white candle and sprinkle a circle of sugar around it. Think about what you'd like to manifest and see yourself having achieved this goal. Perhaps you would like to meet your ideal partner, or find your dream job. Say "Sugar sweet, draw to me my heart's desire, as it should be."

Salt

In medieval times, salt was used as protection against evil spirits. It was scattered outside doors and on window ledges to keep harm at bay. The Japanese still continue this practice, and often sprinkle salt on their doorsteps to prevent intruders. Associated with the earth, salt can be used in spells for protection and strength, although it's not a good idea to eat too much!

TRY THIS

Put a pinch of salt in a black charm bag with a pinch of dried rue or rosemary. Carry the bag when you feel vulnerable and need a confidence boost.

Mustard

This fiery condiment made from mustard seeds is ruled by Mars and is traditionally used for protection. The seeds were often carried when making long journeys, to keep the traveler safe from harm. Today it's used in magic when you need to speed things up, add fire, and protect.

TRY THIS

Spread a little mustard on a cracker or a piece of bread. Use your knife to create a symbol matching your heart's desire: a coin if you need money fast, for example, or a heart shape if it's love you're after. Eat whilst visualizing your wish.

Onions

In medieval times, onions were used to protect the home. They were often cut into quarters and placed either in the corners of each room or on the window ledges. Ruled by Mars, this pungent bulb was revered by the Egyptians, who ate it believing that it would absorb all evil. Today, onions can be used in magic to protect, cleanse, and assist with weight loss.

TRY THIS

When chopping an onion, visualize all your worries slipping from your shoulders. Say "I chop away my cares today. I'm cleansed and free. I enjoy being me!"

Vinegar

Tangy and tasty, vinegar is often added to salads as a dressing for extra "bite." Ruled by the element of fire, it can be used in spells and rituals for protection and also to cleanse the body. Vinegar packs a powerful punch when mixed with other ingredients, such as onion or garlic. In folklore it was considered unlucky to give away vinegar.

TRY THIS

To strengthen your immune system and clear your mind, add a teaspoon (5 ml) of vinegar to a glass of hot water with a generous squeeze of lemon juice. Drink whilst visualizing a bright blue light traveling around your body.

VEGETABLES

Healthy and nutritious, these common vegetables have been used in magical practices around the world, giving a whole new meaning to eating your "five a day!" The simple spells suggested are perfect for those new to kitchen witchcraft and show how simple, cupboard essentials can enhance your life in unexpected ways!

Cabbage

Ruled by the moon, this versatile vegetable has many magical properties. It was believed that eating or wearing cabbage leaves would keep evil at bay, and would also cure insanity. Green cabbage is often used in money-drawing spells, because of its color. If cooked with a sprinkling of basil, it will attract a financial boost. It's also thought that eating cabbage at night can improve your sleep pattern.

TRY THIS

Cook salted cabbage in a little butter, sprinkle with pine nuts, and eat whilst imagining that you're showered with money.

Carrots

The ancients believed that carrots could incite lust and increase fertility, because of their shape and color. Ruled by Mars, they're a great addition to any love spell, and eating them can pep up a flagging libido.

TRY THIS

Eat raw carrots as a snack with a mint dip to improve your love life and attract new admirers.

Celery

Associated with the element fire, celery is said to induce desire and was eaten in ancient times to increase lust. Celery seeds can be combined with candle magic to improve psychic awareness, and the stalks can be eaten whilst performing weight-loss spells. A versatile ingredient, celery can also be used in healing rituals.

TRY THIS

Sprinkle a little celery salt into mushroom soup as it cooks, and say "Open my mind, let my power flow. My psychic abilities expand and grow." Stir the soup whilst repeating the chant, and then eat.

Potatoes

Associated with the earth, potatoes are seen as a powerful protective tool, and were carried by our ancestors to cure illness and ease toothache. They are often used in spells for losing weight and healing ailments. Linked to the moon, potatoes can inspire creativity, love, and compassion.

TRY THIS

Begin to peel a potato. As you do so, visualize yourself looking slim and healthy. See any unwanted weight drop from your frame. Say "As I see, so mote it be!" Use the potato in your cooking and discard the peel whilst repeating the visualization and the chant.

Leek

The leek, the national symbol of Wales, has many magical uses. Welsh soldiers would not only eat leeks but also rub them all over their bodies for protection. Associated with Mars, leeks are thought to increase strength and personal power. Eating leeks can keep evil at bay and help you to feel grounded.

TRY THIS

If you're feeling vulnerable and need a pick-me-up, make a soup from leeks, onions, and potatoes. As you eat, visualize yourself cocooned in a circle of golden light.

Corn

Corn is linked to the earth and the mother goddess. It's associated with fertility, protection, and good luck. In the house, stalks of corn were often draped across mirrors to attract good fortune, and ears of corn were placed in a baby's cot to protect it from evil influences. To increase fertility, place a corncob on your altar.

TRY THIS

Take half a cup of corn and hold it in both hands. Make an offering to the sun and ask for its blessing. Take a deep breath and clear your mind. When you're ready, scatter a handful of dried corn onto a table. Look at any shapes or patterns that emerge, as they may be insights into the future.

Lettuce

It's no surprise that this vegetable is linked to the element water. It's great in diets for weight loss and it's a natural opiate, so it helps with sleeping problems. Because it's associated with the moon, lettuce is often eaten to induce calm, and used to create a peaceful and harmonious atmosphere in the home. It's also used in spells to attract money, because of its color and the size of the leaves.

TRY THIS

For a soothing and refreshing sleep, make a magical tea before bedtime by steeping fresh lettuce leaves in hot water for five minutes. Strain and add a spoonful of honey, then drink.

Beetroot

This vibrant red vegetable, associated with the Greek goddess Aphrodite, is linked to love and passion, and often used in spells for beauty. Eating beetroot is said to improve your natural allure. It can also be used as a dye for food and clothes.

TRY THIS

Take a slice of beetroot in vinegar and cut it in two whilst saying "As one becomes two, my heart is true. May love grow fast, with each day that's passed." Then give one of the pieces to your heart's desire. Alternatively, place the sliced beetroot into a small bowl filled with water and leave for five minutes. Remove the slices and use the water to rinse your hands. Repeat the chant above and then wash your hands in soapy water.

Pumpkin

Associated with the moon and also linked to the mother goddess, pumpkins are a popular Wiccan symbol during Samhain (Hallowe'en). It's thought that the face carved into the pumpkin and the flickering candle within will scare away evil spirits. Pumpkin seeds are eaten in spells for fertility and strength, and can increase virility in men.

TRY THIS

Drizzle a little sunflower oil over some pumpkin seeds and bake in a hot oven for 20 minutes. Eat whilst making a wish for strength and vitality.

FRUIT

One of nature's finest gifts, fruit is a sweet and tasty treat that's packed full of nutrients. Increasing your intake of fruit will enhance any magical diet.

Apple

Easily one of the fruits most commonly used in magic, apples have long been associated with love and beauty. This tasty fruit, which is linked to the beautiful Greek goddess of love, Aphrodite, has been used for centuries in love spells. On midsummer's eve, it was common for a young girl to scoop the seeds from an apple and place them beneath her pillow in the hope that she would dream of her true love. Another popular game was to peel the skin of an apple with a knife in one continuous loop, then throw it over your shoulder; any letters or shapes formed could predict the identity of a future lover.

☆ TRY THIS

Sit beneath an apple tree and eat an apple whilst making a wish for love. Save any seeds from the core and scatter them in a circle around the base of the tree.

Lemon

This powerful fruit, ruled by the moon, can be used in many different ways. Lemons can promote romance when eaten with sugar or in sweet pies and desserts. Used to flavor many sweet and savory dishes, they're a great addition to any meal and can help with healing, friendship, and general happiness. They're also great for using in cleansing rituals.

☆ TRY THIS

Mix a squeeze of fresh lemon juice with a little rose water and massage into the wax of a white candle. Light during a full moon and make a wish for happiness and love.

Orange

This powerful love fruit is often used in rituals to strengthen bonds and promote happiness in a relationship. The scent of an orange can inspire confidence and enthusiasm. It was also believed in western folklore that eating or drinking orange juice could prevent drunkenness. In China, the orange is a symbol of good fortune, and attracts luck.

TRY THIS

Using a pin, carve your initials and the initials of your true love into a piece of orange peel. Carry it with you as a charm to ensure that your love grows.

Lime

Although this zesty fruit is traditionally used in love spells, it has to be used with care. It can promote love, but it can turn it sour if used too liberally. Always mix lime with other fruits and sugar when you want to attract romance. Ruled by the sun, lime is often used in purification rituals and can help to cleanse body and soul.

TRY THIS

Burn lime-scented oil or incense and waft the vapors through every room to cleanse the space and protect your home.

Banana

Bananas grow upward, and so are linked to the element air. It's thought that eating them can help you to tap into your spirituality and develop intuition Because of their shape, they're also thought to increase fertility, particularly in men. The Hawaiians wrap certain foods in banana leaves to protect the food from negative energy.

TRY THIS

Add chopped banana to porridge, and eat first thing in the morning whilst visualizing the day ahead and everything you want to achieve. See yourself reaching your goals successfully and imagine how you'll feel. Say "I reach my aims with light and love. My day is blessed from up above."

Pear

Because pear trees provide fruit for hundreds of years, they're linked to immortality, and the fruit is often eaten to promote long-lasting youth and beauty. Pears are ruled by Venus and linked to the element water. They're light, sweet, and the perfect addition to any love spell.

TRY THIS

Cut a pear in half and rub the flesh over your skin whilst imagining that you're bathed in sunshine. Say: "As I reveal this pear so fruity, so I enhance my natural beauty." Rinse off with warm water for glowing, plumped-up skin.

Raspberry

This tasty fruit, ruled by the planet Venus, is used in magic for love and happiness. Raspberries have a light, frivolous energy that makes them the perfect addition to spells for romance and to attract admirers. They're a great fruit to eat and serve when you want to get flirty and improve your wit and charm. The scent of fresh raspberries also promotes joy and friendship.

TRY THIS

Place a handful of fresh raspberries in the bottom of a cocktail glass, cover with lemonade, a squeeze of fresh lemon juice, and a sprig of mint, and serve to party guests to promote a fun atmosphere.

Strawberry

If you want to attract love, include strawberries in your diet. This lovely fruit is ruled by Venus and also sacred to the beautiful Norse goddess Freya. The scent of strawberries is often used in spells to attract admirers. Eat with fresh cream and share with the one you love for a really indulgent treat to keep your relationship strong.

TRY THIS

To boost your natural allure, mash a handful of strawberries with a tablespoon (15 ml) of honey and massage onto your skin whilst visualizing yourself bathed in pink light. Rinse off in the shower. Eating this concoction has the same effect!

Grape

This tasty fruit has many uses. Associated with the moon and sacred to the Greek god Dionysus, grapes and the wine made from them were often used in celebrations and as an offering to the gods. Grapes were also used as prophetic tools when draped over statues and tombs. Green grapes are linked to money and prosperity, whilst red grapes can assist in love spells.

TRY THIS

To attract more money into your life, keep a handful of green grapes in a wooden bowl with a selection of coins and a piece of paper stating how much money you need. Eat a couple of grapes every day, while giving thanks for all the blessings in your life.

Pomegranate

This fascinating fruit first appeared in Persia, and has been used around the world in a number of traditions. Babylonian warriors believed that eating pomegranate seeds before battle would make them invincible. The pomegranate features in the Greek legend of Persephone, who was lured into the underworld by the god Hades, who offered her pomegranate. On eating six of the tasty seeds, she became tied to his domain for six months of every year. In magic, the pomegranate can assist with protection, strength, fertility, and good health.

TRY THIS

Scatter pomegranate seeds in a circle outdoors and say "These seeds I sow so my strength does grow. I shine with health, divine beauty, and wealth."

SWEET TREATS

Naughty but nice, sweet treats might not be good for the waistline, but in small doses they can be used to sweeten spells and bring great joy.

Chocolate

Popular throughout the world, chocolate comes from cocoa or cacao beans. The Mazatec people of Mexico believed that these beans could attract great wealth. The beans were also used in healing rituals and buried along with parrot feathers, as an offering to the gods in exchange for healing powers. Today, chocolate is used in spells for love and money.

TRY THIS

Break a bar of chocolate into pieces. Every day, take a piece and say "With joy and love I savor this. My world is blessed with happiness."

Cream

Like milk, cream is often used in offerings to deities, and is sometimes eaten during rituals for the mother goddess. Its nurturing properties are linked to the moon, and it's associated with joy and pleasure, hence the phrase "the cat that got the cream," meaning someone who is pleased with him- or herself. Cream can be used in love spells and for general wish-fulfillment.

TRY THIS

On the night of a full moon, leave a saucer of cream outside. Write your wish on a piece of paper, fold it, and leave it beneath the saucer. In the morning, if any of the cream has gone, it is a sign that your wish has been granted.

Maple syrup

Popular with Native Americans, maple syrup is linked to the earth and often used in spells for love and money. Early American settlers recognized its power, and believed that an elixir made from the syrup could cure the common cold. Today, it's a sweet treat that can boost the bank balance and attract new love.

TRY THIS

If you're looking for love, drizzle some maple syrup in the shape of a heart on a pancake and enjoy it for breakfast or use it as part of a recipe for some heart-shaped cookies. Visualize yourself happy and in love as you eat.

Honey

Ruled by the Yoruban goddess of love and beauty, Oshun, honey is a sweet treat with lots of benefits. With its antibiotic properties, it's not only great for the skin, but also can be eaten and used in healing brews for the throat and chest. The Greeks used it as an elixir of youth, and the Egyptians believed that it was sacred and kept it in their tombs. Governed by the sun, honey is today used in magic for love, beauty, wisdom, and health.

TRY THIS

Heat some milk gently and add a spoonful of honey. As you stir, visualize yourself glowing with health and natural beauty. Let the liquid cool and add it to running bathwater, then immerse yourself in the sweet-smelling tub.

Cooking and Baking Tips

The actions you perform in the kitchen are just as important as the ingredients you use. Each one has a specific use or meaning that can enhance your spell work. Think about what you're doing, as you do it. If you're stirring, for example, you're mixing things together to make something new, creating warmth and movement, and encouraging the energy of the ingredients to flow. This makes stirring the perfect time to visualize your intention and to perform spells for some kind of movement or motivation. It's also important to think about the direction you stir in. If you stir clockwise, you're being proactive and attracting things to you; if you stir anticlockwise, you're keeping things at bay.

CHOPPING

When we chop something, we're performing a cutting action, severing something into two or three or four. We're chopping things away and changing the shape of our ingredients. So it makes sense to use chopping when you need to eliminate something from your life. This could be a bad habit, an unhealthy situation, or a person. Taking half of a piece of cheese, carve into it a symbol that represents the thing you need to get rid of. Saying "I chop you away today!," cut off the piece with the symbol on it and either throw it away or eat it.

GRATING

Grating is about taking one large object, such as a block of cheese or a potato, and grating it into lots of smaller pieces, therefore changing its shape and substance. It is the perfect action to complement spells for transformation or change. If you need a little magical help to lose weight, grate a carrot whilst visualizing yourself looking slim and healthy. Use the grated carrot to make a sandwich with some lettuce and a squeeze of lemon juice.

KNEADING

When we knead, we're working the dough roughly to get air into it, and to change the substance, just as we think through problems in an attempt to shed new light on them. Kneading demands muscle power and strength, and facing challenges also requires a certain amount of stamina, so it makes sense to use this time to work through any problems magically. As you knead, imagine that you're smoothing any issues from your life. Repeat the chant "I knead away my problems today!" and visualize obstacles gradually melting away.

ROLLING

When you roll something out, you're smoothing the mixture and creating a shape, easing out any lumps or wrinkles so that the mixture flows together. This makes rolling the perfect magical action to perform in spells for a happy, harmonious atmosphere. If you need to smooth over problems and heal a relationship, bake a pie. Whilst you're rolling out the pastry, imagine that you're ironing out any problems and smoothing the path for future happiness.

POURING

We usually pour sauces or liquids when we're cooking, which means we're working with the element water. When we cover something with a sauce, it's often to enhance its flavor. Pouring is the perfect tool to use in spells that deal with the emotions. Imagine that you're pouring love into your food, and see the desired outcome in your mind. If someone you know is in need of healing, picture them standing in front of you and imagine pouring pink paint all over them. The color pink is associated with love and compassion, so it's almost as though you're drenching them in positive emotions.

BOILING

Need action fast? Boil a pan of water. Boiling is about getting heat quickly, and about bringing something to a head and getting the desired result. So when you boil a pan of water or the kettle, you're inspiring movement. You're adding the element fire to water and creating steam. Boiling is a powerful magical action that can be used in all types of spell, but it works particularly well if you want to promote passion. Boil a pan of water whilst visualizing an exciting love life. Then use the water to make a spicy cinnamon tea, and add a pinch of chili to give your spell extra power.

SPRINKLING

The word "sprinkling" suggests something magical: the idea that we sprinkle a little happiness here and there, spreading the joy around, taking something small and distributing it over a larger area. This makes sprinkling the ideal magical action for general wishes and for spreading love. The next time you sprinkle salt and pepper into your cooking, imagine you're sprinkling love and happiness and that you're infusing your food with extra vitality.

CHAPTER 7

A WITCH'S CALENDAR

The Wiccan Year

Wiccans refer to their calendar as the "wheel of the year," and see it as an ongoing cycle of shifting seasons. There are eight key dates on this wheel. These dates mark celebrations known as "sabbats," each of which has its own special meaning. This usually depends on the time of year when the sabbat occurs, and as you learn more about each festival, you'll notice how deeply embedded they are in the seasons. Wiccans take their lead from the changing environment and the themes covered tend to match what is going on around them. To understand the Wiccan path, it's important to learn about and embrace these festivals.

By thinking about what they mean to you, and doing something unique to mark each one, you'll gain a deeper insight into the craft and be able to tap into the energy of each season. You'll understand the importance of the cycles of life and the need for light and dark, and you'll form a deeper connection with Mother Nature.

Seasonal Celebrations

As a Wiccan, you walk with nature every day. You notice the changing of the seasons and what that means for you and those around you. You feel the rhythm and energy of the earth, and use it to help you to manifest a happy, harmonious environment. Learning about the wheel of the year and the different festivals will help you to attune to Mother Nature, but you can tap into her power at any time. Every day is for celebrating and as you walk the path, you'll create your own rituals and traditions. If one day you notice that the leaves are turning, for instance, you might want to perform an autumnal ritual to mark it. Take inspiration from some of the suggestions in this chapter or come up with your own ideas—it's entirely up to you. That's part of the beauty of the Wiccan path: you find your own way and go at your own speed. So have fun, and give thanks for every day and every step on the journey.

Here is a brief guide to the festivals, including their associations, to help you celebrate and navigate the wheel of the year.

İMBOLC: AROUND FEBRUARY 2

One of the four Celtic fire festivals, sometimes called the "feast of the torches," Imbolc celebrates the rebirth of the sun. The word itself means "in the belly," suggesting that nature is pregnant and ready to bloom. As winter passes, the light returns, and new life is unleashed. It's a time of hope, energy, and fertility; a time to sow seeds for the future, both physically—as our ancestors would have done—and metaphorically—by putting plans into action. Wiccans tend to celebrate this festival by lighting white candles and decorating their homes with fresh spring flowers.

DEITY	Brigid (in her capacity as goddess of poetry and healing)
ALTAR DECORATIONS	Corn dolls, fresh flowers (particularly snowdrops)
HERBS AND SPICES	Cinnamon, ginger, rosemary
COLORS	Orange, white, yellow

İMBOLC RİTUAL

Decorate a box (a shoebox is perfect) in the colors of Imbolc, using ribbons, paper, and pictures of spring flowers. Write your wishes for the coming year on a piece of paper and place it in the box with a sprig of fresh rosemary. Say "As the sun returns and brings rebirth, I give my thanks to Mother Earth. Embracing change, renewing hope, the future seeds of light I sow." Leave the box on your altar or in a prominent place and keep adding your hopes and wishes for the future. Also remember to use the box to give thanks for the good things that are already in your life.

OSTARA: AROUND MARCH 21

Named after the Germanic goddess of the moon and fertility, Eostra/Ostara, this bountiful festival celebrates the natural world coming alive. Spring has truly sprung and fertility abounds. The earth is a myriad of bright colors, from the lush green of the grass to the vibrant flowers in full bloom. Ostara falls on the spring equinox, when night and day are of equal length. This creates the perfect balance between light and dark. The hare, a spritely creature thought to be a messenger between worlds, is also associated with this festival and with the goddess of the same name.

DEITY	Ostara
ALTAR DECORATIONS	Eggs, spring flowers (including daffodils and crocuses), seeds, feathers
SPICE	Nutmeg
COLORS	Green, purple, white, yellow

OSTARA RITUAL

Eggs are a symbol of fertility associated with Ostara. Decorate the shell of a hard-boiled egg using colored pens or paint. Think of a symbol that represents abundance—a flower in full bloom, perhaps, or a star—and draw it on the shell. Bury the egg outside or, if you prefer, in a plant pot of compost, and say "Ostara blessings fall on me, abundance and fertility. As light and dark a balance find, joyful thoughts do fill my mind." Leave the egg buried overnight, then dig it up in the morning and place it on your altar.

BELTANE: MAY 1

Another Celtic fire festival, and the May Day celebration, Beltane is named after the Celtic fire god Bel, whose name means "Bright One." It's a time when nature is at its most fertile, when the maiden aspect of the triple goddess is in full bloom. The earth's powers are at their strongest, and there's a sense of fun and passion to the celebrations. Fires were traditionally lit to honor the sun, and young couples would jump over the fire together as a way of cementing their love; others also jumped the fire, to promote strength and fertility. Livestock were driven through the smoke, in the hope that it would keep them healthy through the coming year. The May King and Queen paraded together, representing the union of sky and earth.

DEITY — Bel

ALTAR DECORATIONS — Rowan (mountain ash), hawthorn, and birch branches, candles, flowers of the season (particularly daisies and roses)

HERB AND SPICE — Rosemary, vanilla

COLORS — Gold, green, pink, red, white

BELTANE RITUAL

Traditionally, couples would also "jump the broomstick" together, to ensure a long and happy union. This is something you can do with your partner, or by yourself to attract love. Lay a broom or brush on the floor. Surround it with a circle of flowers or stones to represent the earth. To begin, say a few words, for example, describing the things you appreciate about each other, then give thanks for the love you have. If you're single, give thanks for all the loving people already in your life, and make a wish for your perfect partner. Jump over the broom, holding hands if you're a couple.

LITHA: JUNE 21–22

Celebrated over the longest day and the shortest night the summer solstice, Litha, marks a turning point in the wheel of the year. The goddess is pregnant and flourishing and the earth is bathed in light, but it's all about to change: the return of the dark is imminent. The god, also known as the Oak King, is about to hand over the baton of power to his twin brother, the Holly King. This is the time of year to celebrate everything you've achieved so far, to embrace joy and to develop a sense of fun. The seasons are changing and winter is on its way, but this shift in balance is needed to keep the wheel turning.

DEITY	All sun goddesses, including the Norse Sunna and the Japanese Amaterasu
ALTAR DECORATIONS	Oak leaves, flowers (particularly sunflowers), bread, honey, yellow and orange candles
HERBS	All herbs
COLORS	Blue, green, orange, purple, red, yellow

LITHA RITUAL

To honor the sun at the height of its power during this summer solstice celebration, rub a little sunflower oil into the wax of an orange or yellow candle. As you do this, think of all the things you'd like to manifest during the rest of the year. When you're ready, light the candle and stand before it. Breathe in and, as you breathe out, imagine pouring your love into the flame, and see it rising up toward the sun. Say "I honor the strength and the power of the sun. I move forward giving thanks for all that is done. Upon this day, upon this hour, I embrace the might of the sun's radiant power." Let the candle burn down.

LAMMAS: JULY 31–AUGUST 1

Named from the words "loaf mass," Lammas is a harvest festival. The union of god and goddess is complete, and the first grain is ready to be gathered in. It's a time to give thanks for the abundant blessings in your life and to reap what you sowed earlier in the year. It's also the festival of Lugh, the Celtic god of light. There's a shift in seasons around this time, and although the sun is still dominant, it's starting to wane, as the wheel of the year turns. Lugh is thought to be the spirit of the grain, and is often linked to the character John Barleycorn, who gives his life just as the grain is cut, so that it may be reborn to sustain the community.

DEITY	Lugh
ALTAR DECORATIONS	Corn dolls, wheat, grain, sunflowers, sunflower seeds, oats
HERB	Mint
COLORS	Gold, green, orange, yellow

LAMMAS RITUAL

Take a handful of corn kernels and some oats in a cup, and scatter them outside. As you do so, say "I give thanks for my blessings, I give back to the earth, as the cycle moves on toward nature's rebirth." Spend some time sitting outside and soaking up the energy of the earth. In your head, list all the things you're grateful for, and then think of all the things you could do to make your world an even better place.

MABON: AROUND SEPTEMBER 21

This great feast gives thanks for the fruit harvest. Just like Ostara, it's held on an equinox, meaning that day and night and light and dark are in perfect balance. Autumnal shades shine in the leaves of the trees and the ripe fruits and vegetables. Although the sun is now waning, and darkness has power over light, it's still a time to celebrate and enjoy the fruit of your labor. It's also time to honor the crone aspect of the triple goddess, and to accept that the descent into the darkness of winter is necessary for the earth to be replenished.

DEITY	Demeter, Hecate
ALTAR DECORATIONS	Seasonal fruit and vegetables, particularly red apples, rosehips, and hawthorn berries
SPICES	Cinnamon, frankincense, juniper
COLORS	Green, orange, purple, red, yellow

MABON RITUAL

At night, leave a bowl of fresh fruit and berries on your window ledge or outside in your yard as a way of honoring the crone aspect of the goddess. On a piece of paper, make a note of anything you'd like to release from your life, such as a pattern of behavior, a painful memory, or a bad habit. Fold the paper three times and place it in the bowl of fruit. Say "Return to the earth, to the darkness below. I bury you deep, I let you go." In the morning, bury the paper in some earth and eat a piece of fruit from the bowl.

SAMHAIN: OCTOBER 31

Also known as All Hallows' Eve or Hallowe'en, the fire festival Samhain is one of the most important Wiccan festivals. It marks the end of summer and the start of the dark half of the year. It's a time to remember lost loved ones and honor the ancestors and is the last of the harvest festivals. The goddess in her crone aspect mourns the death of the god, but also understands that his passing was necessary so that the wheel of the year can move forward. It's thought that at this time of year the veil between worlds is thin, making it easy for spirits to wander and for us to communicate with them.

DEITY	All deities of the underworld (such as Anubis, Kali, Lilith, Morrigan)
ALTAR DECORATIONS	Acorns, nuts, berries (particularly hawthorn), pumpkins, pumpkin seeds, candles, photographs of loved ones who have passed away
HERBS AND SPICES	Basil, frankincense, myrrh, sage
COLORS	Black, gold, orange, purple

SAMHAIN RITUAL

Honor lost loved ones by setting a place at the table for them. Light a black candle and place in front of it photographs of those who have passed away. Gaze at your reflection in a hand mirror. Ask the spirits to bless you with a vision and speak aloud any messages of love. Let the candle burn down, and accept any thoughts or images that come to you—they could be signs from the spirit world.

YULE: DECEMBER 21

The winter solstice is another turning point on the wheel of the year. It is the shortest day, the time when the goddess once more gets ready to give birth to the new sun god. The longest night of winter, often called "the dark night of the soul," it is a time when new hope springs forth. From darkness, the spark of life and light is reborn, and we know that the sun is returning, summer is on its way, and it's time to give thanks. The Romans celebrated Saturnalia at this time, and would decorate their homes with evergreen trees, throw great feasts, and exchange gifts, not unlike the Christians' celebration of Christmas.

DEITY	Brigid (in her capacity as goddess of the hearth)
ALTAR DECORATIONS	A Yule log, sprigs of evergreen trees (such as holly and ivy), mistletoe
HERBS AND SPICES	Bayberry, cinnamon, frankincense, pine
COLORS	Gold, green, red, white

YULE RITUAL

Light a gold candle and burn some frankincense essential oil. Place a sprig of evergreen leaves in a bowl with a couple drops of cinnamon oil and a sprinkling of confectioners' sugar. Sit for a few minutes and imagine that you're in a dark cave. See yourself stepping out of the cave and emerging into the sun. Say "From darkness there is light, as day takes over night. Let love and joy return, let the flame of life burn." Place the sprig of evergreen on a mantelpiece or window ledge where it can be seen as a symbol of hope and a reminder of joy.

CHAPTER 8

MAGIC
AND BEYOND

Continuing on the Wiccan Path

You're well on your way along the Wiccan path. You've got a basic understanding of witchcraft and how you can use it to enhance your world. You'll be feeling positive, energized, and more connected to the earth. So what happens next? Well, it's entirely up to you. This is your journey, and you dictate the pace and direction. You might feel happy to continue on your path as a solitary witch, learning from the landscape, developing your knowledge, and using it along the way when you feel like it. You might want to delve into more complex areas of the craft or do further research into different mythologies around the world and how magic features in each of them. You might want to talk to like-minded people, or join a coven. This is perfectly natural, because you can learn a great deal from others who follow a similar path. Alternatively, you might want to be brave and form your own coven or magical group. There are no right or wrong choices, only options. So whichever direction you choose, here are some tips to help you on your way.

The Solitary Practitioner

There's something special about being a solitary practitioner. It allows you to spend time with yourself, immersed in your own thoughts, so you'll develop highly attuned intuitive skills and get a real understanding of who you are and what you want from life. Solitary practitioners may not shout what they're doing from the rooftops, but they can still make a difference. Many witches work on their own because of circumstance or because they prefer to keep that side of their life private. If you feel happiest following this path, you can still become a powerful spell-caster and reap the benefits of the Wiccan lifestyle.

BOOK OF SHADOWS

This is your bible, your personal journal and chart of all your magical workings. It's where you collect thoughts, ideas, and spells. Most witches start their own book of shadows, writing down ingredients needed for spells, and how to work with them. They also use it as a way of recording their progress. In other words, does this spell work, what were the results, and how might you improve it in the future? You can organize the book in any way you want, listing spells in specific areas or just writing them down as they're needed. Some witches illustrate their book of shadows, and some use it for creative endeavors or to record any psychic impressions.

WICCAN WISDOM

Invest in a hardcover notebook and make it special by customizing the cover with pictures and decorations. Before you use it, perform a special ceremony to inaugurate the book and assist you in your writing. Use something simple like lighting a white candle and placing the book in front of it whilst saying a few words, such as "This book of shadows is the key to all the magic inside of me. The words within enhance my power, from this day on and from this hour." When you've finished, let the candle burn down and wrap the book in black silk, to keep it protected from negative energy.

ALTAR

Most witches have an altar that they use in their magical work. This sacred space is generally used to worship the god and goddess, but it can also be adapted to suit specific needs. For example, if you're performing a love spell, you might decorate the altar with items associated with love, such as a piece of rose quartz, pictures of Cupid, or red roses. A traditional witch's altar is usually the place where the wand, athame, and cauldron are stored, but again this depends on preference. Some practitioners like to have a mobile altar, which they can pull out and create when they need it, rather than having it on display all the time. This is an easy option for the beginner: all you need is a coffee table that is easily accessible, and items that you can put on it to distinguish it as your sacred altar when you want to perform a spell. These might be a special tablecloth, crystals or stones, and magical pictures. It's a good idea to cleanse the area first by burning some oil, or steeping fresh sage in a bowl of hot water and letting the perfumed vapor fill the space.

WICCAN WISDOM

Think about the elements involved in magic, and try to include on your altar something that represents each one. Good examples are a stone or crystal for earth, a candle for fire, and, to represent water, oil and water in a burner, which, once lit, will produce vapor to represent air. Also think about including something that grows, to enhance your connection with Mother Earth, perhaps a vase of fresh flowers or a plant. Something simple like a stick of bamboo doesn't require much attention, and it amplifies energy, so it will help to give your spells extra power.

MAGICAL HELPERS

As a solitary practitioner, you might want to ask for extra help with your spells. This can come from spirit guides, angels, deities, fairies, or elementals. It's a good idea to do some research first and find out which group you're drawn to. Here's a brief explanation of each.

Spirit guides

We all have a spirit guide that helps us throughout our life. Sometimes, but not always, it is a loved one who has passed away. Spirit guides talk to us by sending signs and communicating through our intuition. When you feel something strongly, it is probably a message from your guide. They're particularly useful when you are trying to develop your psychic skills, and will often appear in dreams or visions. Spirit guides can be used for protection and strength, and to help you see into the future.

Angels

Angels exist on a different plane, and there are many types, from the guardian angels we're assigned at birth, to the archangels that we can call upon at any time. Angels are powerful spiritual beings who want to help us, and just need to be asked. It's a good idea to do some research into the different types of angel and the areas they govern. For example, Archangel Michael is a warrior angel and can help you deal with fear and give you confidence and strength in any situation. He is often pictured wearing armor, and blue is the color associated with him. To connect with him, you might visualize being bathed in blue light. Call upon the angels to help in any area of life, simply by talking to them in your mind and giving thanks for all the good things you have.

DEİTİES

Gods and goddesses have been around since the beginning of time. These powerful archetypes feature in mythologies from around the world, and there's a myriad of tales and myths associated with each one, so make a point of doing some research first. You'll probably find that you're drawn to a particular mythology or deity, and this is a sign that their influence is at work in your life, or that you need to work with them. Each deity governs several areas, so make sure you pick one that can help you with your specific request. Look at their associations; they might be pictured with a certain animal, for example, or wearing a particular item of clothing or color. When petitioning for their help, surround yourself with things they're associated with, or make an offering to them. For instance, the Yoruban goddess Oshun loves honey, so her followers would always leave a small spoonful of honey for her as a way of showing their gratitude.

Fairies

Fey spirits often pop up in folklore. These magical beings were thought to exist in another world next to our own. Many tales tell of fairy mounds and other similar locations, which were portals for humans to travel into their land. In some stories fairies are tricksters, who enjoy playing with humans and trapping them with riddles and spells. One thing they all have in common is a sense of fun and frivolity. The druids believe that there are fey spirits attached to every natural thing, and that rocks, stones, flowers, and trees all have a spirit living inside of them. In magic, fairies can help to create a happy, harmonious atmosphere. They love gifts, particularly sweet treats, so if you want them to help you with a spell, leave a few cookie or cake crumbs on a plate near your altar. Because of their strong links with nature, you might want to bring the outside in; yellow flowers in particular are thought to encourage fey beings into the home. They also like music, so hang bells and wind chimes at windows and in doorways.

Elementals

Like fairies, these spiritual beings are associated with the four elements: earth, air, fire, and water. They can powerfully enhance any magic spell that's governed by their element. For example, if you want movement and success, you might choose to work with fire and perform a candle spell, and so you might ask for the help of the salamander elemental. Gnomes are associated with earth, undines with water, and sylphs with air. Ask for their help whilst performing a ritual that focuses on their element. You can also develop a relationship with them over time by giving thanks for their presence in your life. For example, when you take a shower, thank the undines for blessing you with lovely, refreshing water, or when you go for a walk, thank the gnomes for providing the earth beneath your feet.

Joining a Coven

If you'd like to get to know similar-minded folk, you could join a coven. The best place to start is by looking on the Internet and in Wiccan magazines. It's also a good idea to get involved in events in your area, as this is a great way of meeting people and getting to know about different covens. You'll soon discover whether you're on the same wavelength and whether you feel this is something you'd like to pursue. Because many of these groups are well established and have certain traditions and ways of doing things, it might take some time before you're accepted. The group will want to get to know you, and find out how committed you are to the Wiccan path. This might sound scary, but it's the same as with any group or association—they want to know that their members have their best interests at heart. You may be invited along to a special event, sabbat, or ritual so that you can see what it's like to be part of a coven and whether this is the right choice for you. Make sure you ask plenty of questions and get a feel for the energy of the group.

Covens are a great place to develop your magical skills and learn about the Wiccan path. You'll feel fully supported, and you'll be able to ask for help with spells and rituals. You'll feel part of a community, able to celebrate and connect with others at special times, such as festivals and events. Some witches enjoy being part of this family and make deep connections and friendships; others may stay for a while, learning as much as they can about the craft, before returning to solitary practice. Again, there are no rules to dictate the path you take.

FORMING A COVEN

There's something to be said about learning together. If you'd prefer to start from scratch, creating your own coven or magical group could be the path for you. Again, you need to test the water with people you know who might be interested. Start small by having a magical coffee morning where you can talk about your beliefs, laugh together, and form bonds. Make this a regular occurrence, then take it a stage further by suggesting that you meet to celebrate a special event, such as Mabon. If this works, you might want to perform a ritual together to cement your group. This doesn't have to be anything grand—a simple circle with candles and chanting whilst holding hands will suffice, but go for something more complex if you wish. The beauty of forming your own coven is that you can create new ways of doing things and forge your own path. Think of it in terms of any group: you're there to support and encourage one another, whether by listening and offering advice or by doing something active, like performing a ritual together.

Magical Traditions

As you develop your skills and your interest in the Wiccan path, you might like to explore other magical traditions. Oracles, tarot cards, and crystals are all excellent for helping you to hone your intuition, and can be used to give spells a boost. Here's a brief guide to the pastimes linked to the craft, and how to get started.

TAROT CARDS

No one knows the definite origins of the tarot, although there are a number of theories. It's most probable that the use of the cards spread through Europe with traveling gypsies. In Victorian times, tarot became a popular parlor game, which turned into a way of telling the future. Highly symbolic and littered with archetypes, the cards are a tool that can help you to tap into the subconscious mind. Because of their powerful imagery, they can be used in spells to help with visualization.

TRY THIS

If you're thinking of learning more about tarot cards, invest in a pack, and start by acquainting yourself with the images of the Major Arcana. Choose a card a day, and, focusing on the picture, imagine it growing in size until you can step into it and explore. Make a note of any thoughts or feelings that you experience. It's important to form a personal relationship with the tarot before using it with others.

CRYSTALS

Crystals and stones have a specific energy that can be used for healing and in spells. Quartz is popular because it amplifies energy and so works for most types of magic, but a wealth of information is available on the different types of crystal and stone and their various associations. As with any kind of magic, trust your intuition and you won't go wrong.

TRY THIS

It's important to choose stones that you're drawn to, and that feel right, so always pick a stone up before buying and take a few minutes to see how it affects you. If it makes your hand tingle or fills you with a rush of energy, then it's the right stone for you.

PENDULUMS

A pendulum can be made by attaching an object, usually something the practitioner wears or carries with them, to a piece of string or a chain. It is then allowed to dangle and, by asking simple questions to establish "yes" or "no" answers by checking the direction of its swing, it can be used to divine the future. Witches use pendulums when they need a straightforward response to a question, for example, "Should I use candle magic for this spell?" In medieval times, pendulums were often used as a way to tell the sex of a baby. The pendulum was held over the mother's stomach, and various questions were asked to find out if it was a boy or a girl. This tradition is still popular today.

CRYSTAL BALL

Often associated with fortune-tellers and mystics, the crystal ball is an effective scrying tool. It can be used to find solutions to problems or to give insights into the future. The idea is that once you are fully relaxed and tuned in, you fix your gaze on the surface of the ball, and let images form.

TRY THIS

It takes time and practice to perfect the art of scrying, and the most important thing is not to force it. If you don't want to invest in a crystal ball, start with something simpler, like a bowl of water or a mirror. Close your eyes for a few minutes, breathe deeply, and ask the scrying tool to reveal an insight or vision. Open your eyes and let your eyelids droop a little, forcing your eyes to relax. Make a note of any impressions, as these may prove useful for the future.

PSYCHOMETRY

A form of extra-sensory perception, psychometry is the art of reading objects. A psychometrist will pick up an object belonging to a person, and be able to describe character traits and things that have happened or will happen. This tends to work best with a piece of jewelry or something that the person carries with them all the time. It's a useful addition to magical work, and can help you to develop psychic skills and connect with others.

TRY THIS

Invite your friends over and start with a fun party game. Ask them to place an item of jewelry in an envelope whilst you're out of the room. Pick out a piece, close your eyes, and let any thoughts or feelings come to you. You may see symbols or shapes or a word may pop into your head. Try and relate these to the person: if you see a heart, for example, you might say "This person is very romantic." Repeat what you see or feel, and then see how close you were to the truth.

AURA READING

As you develop your psychic gifts and use magical tools more often, you may notice that you're able to read auras. The aura is the energy field around the body, and is split into three different manifestations: the physical aura, the emotional aura, and the spiritual aura. When psychics read auras, they're usually tapping into the physical aura. There are different ways of seeing the aura. Some people find it easy to relax and get a sense of color just by looking at someone, while others feel they intuitively know the colors, or are given messages from the spirit world. Each color within the aura has a meaning—for instance, lots of red might suggest someone who's forceful and angry—but the aura changes constantly to reflect the person's feelings, so it's not an accurate reading of the personality.

TRY THIS

Place a piece of fruit on a dish in front of you, and spend a minute just gazing at it. Notice everything you can about it—the color, size, and shape—then close your eyes for a few minutes and quiet your mind. Breathe deeply until you feel relaxed. Open your eyes and, letting your eyelids relax, focus once more on the fruit. This time, look at the outline and see if you can see any colors developing. You might just get a sense of some kind of energy growing around the fruit's skin. Don't worry if you can't see anything. Reading auras is a skill that needs to be practiced regularly. You can also try this exercise with flowers, plants, and trees, before moving on to friends and family.

Conclusion: The Next Steps in Your Wiccan Journey

The Wiccan path is a personal journey and, as with any journey, you'll learn much along the way, both about yourself and about the world around you. This book is a starting point. A wealth of information is available, from fantastic websites with endless resources, to clubs, societies, and suppliers that can help with any questions you may have. Most importantly, there's the world around you, the environment you live in. Because the Wiccan path is closely intertwined with Mother Nature, much of what you learn will come from this glorious planet, so get outside and explore. Make your own connections with nature and you'll reap the benefits.

Once you learn to look at the world differently, everything falls into place. Take it month by month and note the changes you see around you. What is happening to the environment? What about the creatures that live here? How do you feel in yourself? Some months you'll feel like hiding away, whilst at other times you'll be leaping out of bed with a spring in your step. It's different for everyone, which is why it's important for you to chart your progress through the year. There's a time for everything on the witch's wheel, and you'll begin to notice the subtle changes in nature and in yourself.

Always trust your intuition. The answers you seek are within you—you simply have to learn to tap into your subconscious mind and use the energy around you to make positive change. Ask questions and seek answers through quiet contemplation. If something is right, you'll sense it in your heart and feel the warmth inside. And if something is wrong, you'll feel that, too.

The Wiccan way is kind and caring. Those who follow it take responsibility for themselves and others. So be kind to yourself and anyone you meet along the way. Remember that thoughts are energy, and what you put out will return to you threefold. In other words, get out there and have fun. Let your creative side take over and enjoy the gift of life. Celebrate your achievements and embrace your place in the world.

See magic, be magic, make magic happen!

BLESSED BE!

RESOURCES

FURTHER READING

Rae, Beth, *Hedge Witch: A Guide to Solitary Witchcraft*, (Robert Hale, 1992)

Campanelli, Pauline and Dan, *Wheel of the Year: Living the Magical Life*, (Llewellyn, 1988)

Carding, Emily, *Faery Craft: Weaving Connections with the Enchanted Realm*, (Llewellyn, 2012)

Conway, D.J., *Moon Magick: Myth and Magic, Crafts and Recipes, Rituals and Spells*, (Llewellyn, 1995)

Cunningham, Scott, *Earth Power*, (Llewellyn, 1984)
—*Encyclopedia of Magical Herbs*, (Llewellyn, 1985)
—*Cunningham's Encyclopedia of Crystal, Gem and Metal Magic*, (Llewellyn, 1988)
—*Wicca: A Guide for the Solitary Practitioner*, (Llewellyn, 1988)
—*Living Wicca: A Further Guide for the Solitary Practitioner*, (Llewellyn, 1993)

Duff, Gail, *The Wheel of the Wiccan Year: How to Enrich Your Life through the Magic of the Seasons*, (Ebury, 2011)

d'Este, Sorita, *Practical Wicca and Witchcraft: Towards the Wiccan Circle*, (Avalonia, 2008)

—*Practical Elemental Magick: Working the Magick of Air, Fire, Water, and Earth in the Western Esoteric Tradition*, (Avalonia, 2008)

Farrar, Janet and Stewart, *A Witches' Bible: The Complete Witches' Handbook*, (Robert Hale, 2002)

Hutton, Ronald, *The Triumph of the Moon: A History of Modern Pagan Witchcraft*, Oxford Paperbacks, 1995)
—*Stations of the Sun: A History of the Ritual Year in Britain*, (Oxford Paperbacks, 2001)

Illes, Judika, *The Element Encyclopedia of Witchcraft*, (Harper Element, 2010)

K, Amber, *Coven Craft*, (Llewellyn, 2002)

Jones, Kathy, *The Ancient British Goddess: Goddess Myths, Legends, Sacred Sites and Present Revelation*, (Ariadne Publications, 2001)

Matthews, Caitlin and John, *Encyclopedia of Celtic Wisdom: A Celtic Shaman's Sourcebook*, (Element, 1994)

McCoy, Edain, *Inside a Wiches' Coven*, (Llewellyn, 2003)
—*A Witch's Guide to Faery Folk: How to Work with the Elemental World*, (Llewellyn, 2002)

Moura, Ann, *Grimoire for the Green Witch: A Complete Book of Shadows*, (Llewellyn, 2012)

Newman, Paul, *Lost Gods of Albion*, (Sutton Publishing, 1999)

Riddle, Kirsten, *Channel Your Goddess Energy*, (CICO, 2013)

Silja, *The Green Wiccan Book of Shadows*, (CICO, 2011)

Valiente, Doreen, *Natural Magic*, (Robert Hale, 1999)

West, Kate, *The Real Witches' Coven*, (Element, 2003)

Wedeck, Harry, *The Dictionary of Magic*, (Golden Press, 1976)

Worwood, Valerie, *The Complete Book of Essential Oils and Aromatherapy*, (New World Library, 1991)

WEBSITES

www.botanical.com
Fantastic herbal encyclopedia.

www.paganfed.org
A great starting point for contacts and a general understanding of the craft.

www.thealmanack.com
Gives you the current moon phases, planets that rule certain days, etc. Provides a helpful monthly, printable page.

www.witchcraft.org
Brilliant site with resources, information, contacts, events, and everything you need to embark on the Wiccan path.

www.witchvox.com
Extensive site for all things Wiccan, with a focus on events in the US.

www.witchfest.net
A comprehensive calendar of Wiccan events and gatherings.

İпdex